Nick Jenkin was born in London. After teaching in the East End and the West Country, he went onto study Philosophy at Sussex University.

Amongst other things he worked as a merchant seaman, a teacher in Wormwood Scrubs, a shoe salesman in Regent Street, a canoe instructor, a painter and decorator, a manager of a Citizen Advice Bureau and then with young offenders and homeless youth. He finally settled into a career as a Citizen Advocacy manager, supporting the rights of adults with learning disabilities.

As well as being politically active, he sang with 'The Chorus of The National Orchestra of Wales' for 8 years and with other choirs in Cornwall, Ireland, France and Palestine.

He now lives in Greece with his wife, Nancy.

Dedicated to Nancy, my co-rider, and to
Wilson and Sandy for finding it amusing in the first place!

Nick Jenkin

NICK AND NANCY TAKE A TRIP

AUSTIN MACAULEY PUBLISHERS™

LONDON • CAMBRIDGE • NEW YORK • SHARJAH

A CIP catalogue record for this title is available from the British Library.

ISBN 9781528937399 (Paperback)
ISBN 9781528969086 (ePub e-book)

www.austinmacauley.com

First Published (2020)
Austin Macauley Publishers Ltd
25 Canada Square
Canary Wharf
London
E14 5LQ

It Seemed Like a Good Idea at the Time

Nick – It was about a year ago that we decided we needed a form of transport to get around the island.

You see, a year before that, in 2015, against all advice, Nancy and I sold up shop in England, bought a house in Greece and moved to live there, lock stock and barrel. We chose the island of Symi.

It is a beautiful little island, set in the blue Aegean Sea, in Southern Greece. The people are as warm as the sun and made us feel especially at home. We took lessons in Greek and when we tried out our fumbling sentences on them, it was the source of much amusement, but the fact that we had tried really seemed to help.

Nancy – Why Symi? Well, I met Nick there 12 years earlier and the island holds many strong feelings for us – of discovering a soulmate, falling in love, holding hands for the first time, that first kiss; and it was all wrapped up in sunshine, sparkling blue sea and happiness.

Nick – I am sure it must have had something to do with all the wine that flowed. It was a singles holiday. Can you believe it? I can't. I was single and so regularly went on holiday with a mate of mine. He was terribly good company but this time he decided he was going to California to drive the coast road on a Harley.

As a single man, I find it very difficult going on holiday on my own. I'm not much of a joiner. In the tavernas and restaurants, everyone feels sorry for you, and as for lying on the beach, well you are a pariah, a predatory male with a 30-foot space around you.

And as if anyone meets a soulmate on a singles holiday! One look at all possible options and you know you are doomed to 2 weeks of solitary misery. But the advert for this singles holiday sounded different. Twelve people, over 25, who stay in a big house, on a hill, overlooking the harbour and all you had to do was eat evening meals together that were especially cooked for you. The clincher – as much wine as you could drink, thrown in free. For the rest of your holiday, you had no obligation to spend time with anyone else, the day was yours to do with as you pleased.

But there she was, standing on the ramp to the ferry, looking shy but intelligent, self-contained but sociable.

Nancy – Nick told me later that he saw me straight away and, when the ferry was underway, he went around and introduced himself to everyone on the holiday just so he could stop and talk to me. How flattering!

I didn't think that I would meet anyone either, but Nick was funny, interesting, kind and seemed to like me! We married a year later, to the month.

But then jump 10 years to our anniversary and we decided to return to Symi just to see what it was like. We had very low expectations because, of course, islands develop and the magic dies but it was as if we had never left. No towering skyscraper hotels, no dreadful disco's beating into the night, just the same Symi. We went back to the place where I had lost my camera, because we couldn't stop kissing and had got all dizzy, but it wasn't there! Then we visited the spot where we first held hands and I thought immediately, we could make a home on Symi.

Nick – Actually there had been some building developments on the island but the regulations are so strict that we couldn't tell. Any new houses looked just like the ones that had been there for years, centuries.

Symi is an irregular shape, like a large hibiscus flower that has floated down from the sky and settled on the sea. It is about 8 miles east to west and 5 miles across, with most of its 2,500 people located at the eastern end in a village, on top of a mountain, which then tumbles down into the sea.

Our house is in a quiet bay called Pedi. It faces the sun and dangles its feet in the sea but here is the draw back. To go to the shops, to a restaurant or simply for a glass of wine, it is a mile up the mountain to the old village and then another mile down to the more bustling harbour.

In summer, our quiet bay boasts 2 tavernas, 2 shops and a small hotel and there is an hourly bus service which serves us well but in winter everything closes. The bus takes a siesta in the afternoon, stops at 8 in the evening and on Sundays it is only active till midday, just long enough to transport the faithful to and from the churches.

Hold on, you might say, there is a kiosk for emergency supplies. Yes, Giorgo is very long suffering and sits there all day waiting to sell you cigarettes, alcohol, biscuits or sweets, which is wonderful if you want to smoke or drink yourself to death but not if you've forgotten the milk.

In winter, the beach reverts to a boatyard and the locals stop fishing for tourists and start fishing for fish. It is wonderful because all the tourists have gone home, and the island reverts to being itself. The only drawback is that forgotten carton of milk. Then it is a mile walk up to the shop or a wait for the bus. Woe betide you if you fancy going out for an evening meal. Then you have to break off at 8 for the last bus or face a walk home, up and over the mountain.

Hence, after the first winter we decided we needed independent transport and that's when the fun started. What kind of transport?

I was all for a scooter, the more common means on the island of getting from A to B.

Nancy – I wanted a car. There are fewer cars on the island but in the depths of winter it would keep us warm and dry and we could offer a lift to our friends and neighbours. Nick wanted a scooter so he could pretend he was a Greek man and show off around the island.

Nick – I wanted a scooter because it is easier to manoeuvre through the narrow lanes and to take to other islands, on the ferry, for jaunts. And as for the summer months of the year, driving a car on the island is like driving an oven, even with the windows open. The decider – scooters are cheaper to buy and cheaper to run. So…

Nancy – So, I was overruled.

Nick – I don't think that is fair. We did discuss it at length.

Nancy – Then I was overruled.

Nick – Anyway, our Greek tutor said – never buy a second-hand scooter because it will be thrashed to within an inch of its life, always buy new.

Now, the nearest place to our island to buy a new scooter is Rhodes but all the models I saw there were Vespas which, to my mind, were absolutely boring. I would be buying something practical but not something I liked or wanted. My view is, if you are going to do something, do it in style.

The other argument was that the new Vespas cost around 4,000 euros, £3,500 at the current exchange rate, which I thought was way overpriced. Also, I had secretly been surfing the net and seen a beautiful, retro scooter for sale at a mere £1,250, new. It was an AJS Modena, 125 cc. AJS is a good make with a good British tradition behind it but these little scooters were made, you've guessed it, in China and simply assembled in Britain!

Nevertheless, it was a saving of – well you work it out. The problem was, that as far as I could tell, it was only for sale from outlets in England, one in France and one in Italy. If I really wanted this bike I would have to work out a way to get it from England all the way to our island in Greece.

More difficult than that, I was going to have to convince Nancy that this was the bike for us.

Nancy – This is where Nick loses it and goes off on one of his fancies. For example, when we got married 14 years ago he had the bright idea of hiring a white horse to carry me to the church. Any sensible person would have chosen a horse and carriage but no, for Nick it had to be a romantic white charger bringing his princess to be wed. Romantic yes, practical no. When I got on the horse, cameras flashed, the horse reared up and I slid to the ground, very gracefully without showing any underwear, according to my mother, but scraping my leg. I ended up limping to the church and arriving late. The new high heels may have contributed to the limping.

Nick – Nancy is correct of course. I got it wrong, but if it had worked it would have been a memorable moment, for the right reasons.

So, this plan to get the bike I wanted had to be good, watertight, make sense and, above all, be attractive to Nancy. But how to get a scooter all the way from England to an island in Greece and still save money?

1. By road?

Well that would mean driving 2,300 miles through France, Belgium, the tip of Holland, Germany, the Czech Republic, Slovakia, Hungary, Serbia, Bulgaria and Turkey, and at the end of it I was not sure we could get a ferry from Turkey to Symi. Moreover, there was no way we could drive 2,300 miles, at 40 to 50 miles an hour. First of all, it would be a mammoth marathon that would take weeks and cost an arm and a leg in hotel bills, secondly, by the time we reached Greece, the scooter would be knackered and thirdly, and more importantly, Nancy would never go for it – hour after hour sitting on the back of a bike. She would simply leave me to it and catch a plane. If we were going to do it, it had to be attractive to Nancy – an adventure, something we could share and that would make good memories. So, driving it overland was out.

2. Shipping it, in a box?

Well, where is the fun in that? It was the most practical option but I was glad when it proved to be more expensive than expected. Also, I had real difficulty finding a company that would dare to take it anywhere beyond the Greek mainland. You would think that the Greek islands are in the back of beyond and, I suppose, in some people's minds they are! So, that was out.

3. The best option was a ferry from the English coast all the way to Greece.

They don't exist.

When we first came to Symi to live, we drove the car over. It was loaded with household goods: TVs, computer, CDs, clothes, bedding, crockery, cutlery and so on. That proved to be great fun. We took our time moseying down through the French countryside, along the French Riviera, stopping at Assisi in Italy then finally caught the ferry to Greece. It would be possible to do it on the little scooter but it would still ask more than 1,000 miles of it, even if we caught the ferry from Venice, in the north of Italy. The journey would be onerous and, at the end of it, we would still have one half-knackered bike let alone knackered backs. However, as it stood, it was the best bet.

Then I had an idea.

Nancy – O dear!

Nick – Option number 4. Euro Star would get us from London to Paris and save miles.

No, it wouldn't. They only take motor vehicles from Folkestone to Calais, just the hop across the channel, well, under it in fact! Euro Star would save us no road miles and, when I looked, it cost about £80. Gosh, we could take the ferry for less than £30 and get the sights and sea air for free!

It was then I discovered a site on the net which described the motor rail routes in Europe but, sadly, most of the old, romantic trains had been scrapped. What on earth would Poirot make of that?

But some remained, even though they only ran during the summer months when they could make a profit, and one of these ran from Dusseldorf in Germany to Verona in Italy. Dusseldorf is only 300 miles from London and Verona only 70 miles from Venice where we could catch the boat to Greece! Hmm, this was beginning to look interesting.

Nancy – The man's a fool but, I suppose I have to say, he never gives up on an idea!

Nick – Yes! Well, if I put my sensible hat on, the cost of the motor rail fare with a private couchette for 2, including the scooter, made the price of the AJS scooter more than if I bought a Vespa in Rhodes. Where was the logic in that?

I priced it up – with an evening meal for 2, the train alone came to over 500 euros, £440. That's a lot of dosh. However, Nancy would love it. A romantic overnight express hurtling through the heart of Europe, a cosy cabin for 2, a meal in the restaurant car, a murder in the next carriage and Poirot investigating. She wouldn't be able to resist. (I lied about Poirot and the murder.)

Nancy – Okay, it was beginning to sound interesting. The sleeper train was making the idea of sitting on the back of a slow, cold scooter, wrapped in leathers, for mile after mile, a little bit more attractive. And I have never been on a motor rail or a sleeper train before, nor eaten in the restaurant car of a train. Neither had Nick. How exciting! I was already beginning to think about who I could nominate to be murdered! But 500 euros?

Nick – Yes, it was pretty steep but it would not only save us 650 miles driving, that is 16 hours or 2 to 3 days on the scooter, but also save the cost of overnight stops into the bargain.

The imaginary journey would go something like this

1. drive to Dover
2. catch the ferry across the channel
3. drive to Dusseldorf to catch the train
4. hop from Verona to Venice
5. then catch the ferry to Greece.

This was beginning to sound feasible, but the cost was still prohibitive. £450 on top of the £1,250 pounds for the bike, then 3 or 4 overnight stops in hotels, the price of the channel ferry, the long ferry trip from Venice to Greece and the ferry from Athens to Symi, oh, and the petrol! It all added up to loads of money. Nearly as much as the boring Vespa in Rhodes!

I gazed longingly at the internet site, "treinreiswinkel.nl." (Train Shop, Nederlands), a Dutch company. Well done the Dutch. There was this fantastic picture of a train, loaded with bikes and cars, speeding through the beautiful European countryside, vines and mountains in the distance, and I wanted it.

It was then, while I was trying to find the cheapest date to travel, I noticed that on the very first day of the service, 19 May, and on the very last day of the service, 30 September, they had special offers, probably because, unlike us, no one wants to travel just one way. I priced it up and the sleeper, motor rail journey came to only 300 euros including the meal and the scooter, which travelled for just 9 euros. That was only £260. It had to be a mistake.

So, I phoned them up. They were brilliant. No press button 9 for option 6, a live person answered straight away and was efficient, spoke English perfectly and confirmed my findings.

But, alas, I couldn't book now. The timetable and prices for the following year, 2017, didn't officially open until much later, around Christmas. I got the date and spoke to Nancy. Did she fancy an exciting adventure, relaxing on the back of a beautiful, special scooter as we wended our way across Europe?

Nancy – No.

Nick – It would be fun, tootling through the countryside with the air on our faces, 3 exhilarating ferry trips, a special couchette on an overnight train, with a delicious meal and I would throw in a special bottle of wine.

Nancy – What am I letting myself in for? The last time I was on the back of a bike with Nick was on our honeymoon in Naxos, another Greek island. I didn't do very well. Every time he leant to go around a bend I leant the other way, to counter his weight. Of course, that was wrong, although it seems very sensible to me. Also, I felt very vulnerable as there was nothing behind me to stop me falling off. I kept imagining Nick turning around to see me gone.

Nick – Nonsense. Nancy was very good. It was just a learning experience. Eventually she agreed to grab me round the waist and stick herself to my body like glue. I couldn't breathe but I held on until we stopped at some deserted dunes, on the other side of the island, where we worked out our differences!

I think it might have been the offer of the bottle of wine that swung it, but Nancy was tentatively on board, so to speak, and everything was under way. All I had to do now was wait until the end of the year, book the train, buy the scooter and the adventure across Europe was on.

Nancy – I didn't actually agree. To be honest, I thought by the time Christmas arrived, Nick would have forgotten all about it and another option would have arisen. But it did sound like quite an adventure.

September 2017,
Let the Games Begin

Nick – We bought the scooter and had it delivered to my sister's place in Barnes, London.

Of course, that was not without its problems. Between the time I began to look and the time I wanted to buy the scooter, they had introduced a new model. It was exactly the same as the old model except they had tweaked the emissions and for this honour they had upped the price by 250 pounds.

I spent weeks on the net and phone trying to find an outlet that still had last year's model at last year's price and felt pretty smug when I succeeded.

My sister is very kind and long-suffering. I suppose that comes from spending a lifetime in the same family as me! She had the bike taken around the back of her apartment and parked safely in the garden. She had been emptying the shed and had the clever idea of arranging hundreds of unwanted flowerpots all around the bike so that any hapless, night-time robber would not only have to navigate the locked gate, the side passage, and the dog but also crunch their way through hundreds of clay pots, let alone deal with my sister in her nightdress, curlers and rolling pin! I almost felt sorry for them.

Come September we left Symi, ready for our adventure. We flew to England, arrived at my sister's apartment, went around the back into the garden, and lifted the cover off the scooter. Would it be all it looked, would it be damaged in transit, would it work?

It was a beauty. Red and white with lots of chrome, just like the ones I used to drive in the '60s along Brighton sea front. Even Nancy fell in love with it.

Nancy – Nick never had a scooter in the '60s and was never a mod.

Nick – Well I could have been. I was, in my fantasies. The fact is, Mods and Rockers happened in the early '60s when I was too young to drive either a scooter or a motorbike. Whatever, Nancy was won over and immediately insisted on sitting on the back to try it out.

Nancy – I was still worried about falling off but Nick had ordered a box to be fitted on the back. It was red and white, just like the bike, and had a neat little curve in it to support my back.

Nick – So far, so good. But the blasted thing wouldn't start. Brilliant. So much for a jaunt across Europe! It was all planned and paid for but the integral part, the scooter, wouldn't start. We tried several times but all it did was cough. It looked good but didn't work! I would sue the company. Hell!

Nancy – I peered into the tank, it had been delivered on fumes.

Nick – She's good! I fetched some unleaded from the petrol station down the road and poured it in. Then we held our breaths. It started first time. Result! Perhaps I wouldn't sue the company after all.

Just to explain: when we are in Greece my sister has the car but when we return to the U.K. for a week or 2, it is at our disposal. We had 2 days to spare so we did the usual round of visits: to Nottingham to see Nancy's mother and family and then to Isleworth, in London, to visit my other sister.

Unfortunately, my other sister is now in a home suffering from Alzheimer's. It is always a shock to see her because she was such a vibrant woman when she was younger. We visit whenever we are in the country and take photos and goodies to eat. This time it was baklava.

From Barnes to Isleworth is only a round trip of 10 miles but this was the chance to try out the scooter on the road. Would I remember how to ride a bike? Would I be able to negotiate the London traffic unscathed?

Nancy, rather worryingly, decided against practicing on the pillion. The first time she would ride the bike would be when we set off on the actual journey, the next morning. I was a little perturbed. Was she beginning to get cold feet?

Nancy – It was the first time Nick had driven the scooter and I thought it would be better for him to practice first, without a passenger. But, to be honest, I was also a bit nervous of being in the busy London traffic. We had planned to leave London for Greece early the next morning, so I wanted my first time on the scooter to be when it was quieter, with less traffic to bump into and less people around to laugh at me.

Nick – When I was 16, I had a BSA 175cc. It was exactly at the time when they introduced the crash helmet law. One minute I was swishing along with the wind blowing through my hair, I had more then, and the next I was imprisoned in a helmet. I couldn't hear properly, I couldn't see half as well and I looked like a proper twerp.

Yes, I know, it was for my own good. All the adults around me at the time made that abundantly clear. If I fell over the handlebars onto my head I would miraculously survive. Also, they would say, think about all the trouble it would be for the other road users and the poor ambulance workers who would have to scrape me up off the road, and the hospital workers, the police…but I never quite agreed about my loss of choice.

Greece, like Britain, also has a nanny state. It passes silly laws telling you what you can and can't do as if you are unable to decide for yourself. But one of the things I love about Greece is that sometimes the Greek people simply ignore the laws. For example, the law says all Greeks must wear a crash helmet but do they heck. On Symi, and even on Rhodes, people decide for themselves. Very few people wear a helmet unless they are a tourist on a hire bike.

When we are in Rhodes, Nancy and I often go to a place called 'The Ronda' for lunch. It was built in the thirties by the Italians who, ahead of their time, designed it as a leisure complex with a yacht club, restaurant and an organised beach complete with changing facilities and art deco diving platform, (think "Death in Venice" swimming costumes). The main circular building has been transformed into a modern and airy coffee lounge, overlooking the sea. The point of this story, however, is that on the door there is a large sign clearly stating "No Smoking" whilst inside people just choose to ignore it and decide for themselves. It's the same in lots of places all over Greece, even though the government is trying to clamp down on smoking in public places.

Now don't get me wrong, smoking is deadly. Neither Nancy nor I want to passive smoke. If the domed ceiling in The Ronda didn't evacuate the smoke, we wouldn't go there. But every time we visit I am brought to laughter simply by the Greek's cool indifference to the law. If I were a smoker with my British upbringing I very much doubt I would have the nerve to just ignore the sign and light up whereas the Greeks simply seem to get on with it. I suppose the fact is, I quite admire how relaxed many of them can be about such things. They don't seem to be so uptight as me when I am in England. Something comes over me and I turn into a tight-assed twit – 'It's past 10 o'clock at night and those people are making too much noise!', 'Why hasn't that house taken in their waste bin, it's making the whole street look untidy?' and so on.

I know this opens up a whole, wide-ranging discussion, so…on with the story.

I felt competent on a bike, with or without a helmet. Apart from the Beezer 175, I had owned a Honda 50 when I was teaching in Devon, remember them? What a racket. And a Suzuki 125 when I worked in London. I loved the Suzuki, it had style. It was metallic red and looked a bit like a small Harley. I had also hired lots of bikes while on holidays.

So, the traffic on the way to Isleworth wasn't too heavy. I wobbled a bit to start with and probably travelled too slowly for the London traffic but the journey was uneventful and I thought I did okay for an old fogey.

While we were visiting my sister, we tried to explain to her about the scooter and the excitement of taking it across Europe but her Alzheimer's meant she didn't really understand. She didn't even want to go outside to look at it.

All she wanted to do was lay on her bed and eat goodies. Indeed, it is all we can do to help her understand that we live in Greece. We show her photos and send her postcards but I'm not sure how much gets through. I wish I could transport her to Symi and sit her in the shade outside our house for a week but, sadly, all that is in the past for her.

Nancy – The thing about adventures like this is that one must be fully prepared. If you know what's coming round the next corner, literally or otherwise, fewer things will leap up and take you by surprise.

So, I made a list of all the equipment we needed to buy, to travel lawfully through Europe and here it is: apart from helmets with visors, (which incidentally we had bought on a school outing to the island of Syfnos) we needed: hi-viz jackets, 2 breathalysers, a GB sticker on the rear of the bike near the number plate, a headlight sticker to deflect the beam, a spare bulb set, 4 luminous flashes on our helmets, boots that cover your ankles, coats that cover your arms, trousers that cover your legs, and, of course, gloves.

When we travelled to Britain, we knew we would be returning to Greece on the scooter, which meant we would be limited in what we could carry. Nick had the box fitted on the back of the scooter, but the rest had to be carried on my shoulders, in a rucksack. So, both of us only brought 2 changes of clothes intending to wash them as we went. We had coats in England but neither of us had boots that covered our ankles, when do we wear them in Greece? So, I bought myself a lovely pair of brown, leather, knee-length boots, out of necessity of course!

Nick – Of course, dear!

Nancy was brilliant at the planning stage. We had pored over maps and the internet, gauged distances and timing, firmed up the route to Symi and booked the hotel for the first overnight stop.

Day one was the most difficult. We would drive from London to Dover, take the ferry to Dunkirk, then drive to our motel just outside of Ghent in Belgium.

We were nervous! There were so many immeasurables. Would the scooter hold up or fall apart? Would I be able to drive in all weathers? Would Nancy be able to endure the journey? Would the rucksack, she was carrying, rest comfortably on the box or weigh down mercilessly on her back? Had we allowed enough time between destinations? Would we be able to find our way across Europe without the benefit of the car sat-nav?

Wet weather was my greatest fear. If it rained it would not only thoroughly drench us but, more importantly, slow us down. And it was a potential killer. Wet roads meant slippery surfaces. It also meant that my visor would mist up and I wouldn't be able to see where I was going so clearly. Just as important, was the fact that other vehicles bearing down on us wouldn't be able to see us so clearly. In short, rain would demand total concentration, bring on tiredness and would turn the whole adventure into a nightmare.

The train out of Dusseldorf left at 6pm on Friday evening. We planned to leave London at 6am on Thursday morning and rain was forecast for Wednesday night!

Into the Unknown

Nick – Wednesday morning didn't dawn as much as dribble in. We both slept fitfully. I remembered in the middle of the night that the Europe road atlas was in the boot of the car and indeed was too big to fit in the box on the back of the scooter or in the rucksack. Anyway, they were both full.

Nancy – I realised that the shoes we had been wearing would have to be left behind, for the same reason. We had to wear our ankle-covering boots so no room for other shoes.

Nick – In the darkness of 6.15am, on the morning of September 29th, we turned ourselves out onto the gravel drive of my sister's apartment. Mercifully, the rain had stopped but all around us were pools of standing water and the bushes were dripping. We uncovered the scooter which, like us poor thing, was still fast asleep. We had made a trial run of packing the bike the evening before, but we forgot that we had to fit in the bike cover as well. So, we found ourselves in one of those ridiculous moments – you know, all of a sudden it's like you see yourself from above and realise how absolutely absurd life is. It was the first of many on the trip. In the murky grey of the London morning, there we both were, hanging on the back of the box, trying to squeeze in the cover at the same time as getting it to click shut. No click no trip. Finally, sighs all round, click.

Nancy – So much for being fully prepared! But I think I am good at organising and had collected together all the important papers, down to the last detail. It made me feel calm, checking and double-checking the documents for each leg of the journey. So, I had all the tickets, the first hotel booking, passports, bankcards, money and maps in my shoulder bag which we managed to bundle into the small compartment under the seat.

Nick – I went to the car, found the road atlas and tore out the relevant pages for our route across Europe so that Nancy could include them in her 'important' bag. Lacking a sat-nav, I had made detailed, drawn maps of how, for example, to get out of Dunkirk, how to find the hotel on the first night and where the station was in Dusseldorf, and they were in her bag too.

What neither us is owning up to is, there is a little lockup box on the side of the scooter and in there we had stuffed tea bags, not only for the journey but to last us at home. We laughed at expats who insisted on watching Coronation Street on the internet or had cornflakes flown in, but here we were carrying our own supply of tea bags. How pathetic is that!

I had a last look at the map to Dover – M25, M20, A20. We togged up, I pressed the starter, and it started. Then we pulled to the edge of Castlenau, in Barnes, a main artery road into London. We had hoped we might miss the London traffic but already it was gearing up for a busy day and was kicking out spray. I heard Nancy behind me mutter to herself, 'OK. You can do this. You have to.'

Nancy – I knew I would be nervous about being on the scooter. However, this is what we had decided to do, so I set my mind to it. *I just have to get on with it,* I thought. And that was that. A little prayer did no harm either.

Nick – We lowered our visors, pulled out into the traffic and were on our way.

As we headed out, I thought, *What the hell am I doing here? I'm an old man. We have a long and arduous journey ahead of us. Seven days of tussling with the unknown. Why aren't I in bed slowly waking up to a nice cup of tea before making our way to Heathrow and a comfortable flight to Rhodes?*

My sister waved us off, poor thing. She would also have preferred to be in her nice, warm bed. I had said to her the day before, 'Why do I do this to myself? Why don't I just give in and sit on a sofa with my feet up?'

She was great. She replied, 'Do it while you can. It's an adventure! Anyway, sitting on a sofa wouldn't be you, would it.'

I wished I had bought the sticker I had seen and stuck it on the back of bike – "Adventure Before Dementia."

We crossed Barnes Common, the rain dripping from the horse-chestnut trees, and made our first stop at some traffic lights. We wobbled but pretended we were seasoned bikers. Pulling away from the lights I grabbed the middle of the road so the car behind me couldn't squeeze us into the gutter. My old dad used to say to me, when you are on a motor cycle boy, he always called me boy even when I was 40, pretend you are a car. Imagine you are sitting in the centre of a car-size space so that the cars behind you can see you, respect your space and don't try to push you off the road. Well it worked, except for a few idiots who just couldn't bear being stuck behind us and thought their place was in front of us, no matter what it cost. Nancy held me tight around the waist and I must say it was an unexpected bonus. We were togged up to the nines in our gear but immediately, with Nancy's arms around me, it was like I was leaning back into a warm armchair. Except for my knees, they were freezing. The list of essentials said nothing about leg warmers.

Nancy – I'm not sure I like being compared to a warm armchair, thank you, Nick. I see myself more as a nubile young woman!

I hadn't realised how cold it would be either. Luckily, I was being sheltered by Nick's bulk.

Nick – And I don't see myself as bulky, thank you.

The drive from Barnes, in South West London, to Dover was just under 100 miles and, according to the net, would take just under 2 hours.

Well that is in a car. How long on a wobbly, slow scooter? We held long discussions about whether we should buy a flexi-ticket for the channel ferry, thereby allowing us as much time as we needed, or whether we should buy a fixed time ticket which cost much less but put a deadline on us. In the end, we decided on the fixed ticket for the midday ferry. If we left London at 6am that would leave us 6 hours to make the journey, surely enough time.

Our first big challenge was the M25. Now I am sure that, for seasoned bikers, it is much the same as any other motorway but for me, even as a car driver, it has always been a mad, lorry laden, racetrack. A filthy, noisy artery that changes in size from 3 to 4, to 5, even 6 lanes, then down to 3 again. Here we were on our little red and white scooter, stuck defiantly in the middle of the inside lane, with dirty, grey juggernauts bearing down on us like modern dinosaurs, filling the rear-view mirrors before swerving at the last minute to overtake. As they pulled alongside, the air they displaced pushed the bike sideways towards the hard shoulder and then, when it passed, the vacuum sucked us back in behind them. The worst were the double trailers, one lorry pulling another, many of them from Eastern Europe. They were like trains. Just as you thought the worst was over along came a second. I was pulling right as they burst alongside then left so as not to swerve in after them.

I couldn't ask Nancy if she was coping okay because of the din – the scooter engine, the traffic, the road noise. If I turned my face slightly the wind tugged at my helmet, jerking my head sideways and my visor upwards, and the surface muck from the night's rain was spraying into our faces, reducing visibility. It was teeth gritting time.

Man or mouse, squeak up boy!

I decided to turn into the first service station I saw. Time to take a break. Time to rub our frozen knees, shake the pins and needles out of my throttle hand and assess our journey so far, a whole hour.

Nancy – I managed to keep my eyes open most of the time, even on the corners. I just held on to Nick and leant with him. But I didn't like the lorries and my legs were beginning to ache from being in one position all the time. There was only a slim portion of the footplate that was allocated for my feet.

Nick – It was as we pulled into the service station that we had our first accident.

We steered around the tight bend into the car park just as the light was turning from dark grey to light grey. We had coffee on our minds. Underfoot the tarmac was greasy – a slick of oil, rain and road residue. I pulled up in front of the cafeteria doors and turned off the engine with a sigh of relief.

At this point, however, my left foot lost purchase on the grease and began to slide away under the weight of Nancy and the scooter. Accordingly, the scooter began a slow fall leftwards. I held on, struggling to keep it upright, my left foot slid further away until I was doing the splits. Despite all this, Nancy simply sat on the back of the scooter with her feet still on the running board like the queen herself. Finally, finding myself thrown across the muck on the tarmac, I looked back to see her still sitting happily on the saddle, her feet neatly tucked onto the running board, as the bike fell over, in slow motion. When it came to rest on its side, she was still astride the scooter, her feet still on the running board and still in a sitting position, except now she was horizontal, on the ground.

That was it. I got the giggles. Then she got the giggles. Another one of those absurd moments. Two grown-ups, who should know better, lying on the slimy ground in a service station, somewhere on the M25, at 7.15 on a dirty September morning. It was just so ridiculous!

Nancy – I don't know what it was. I think I must have fallen asleep. We had never discussed when I should put my feet down. I suppose I thought I had to wait until Nick told me to. How stupid is that? But the incident helped me in some way because now we had had our first 'accident' the whole journey didn't seem so unreal.

A man came over and asked if he could help. Very nice of him but when he saw we were okay even he couldn't stop laughing.

We picked the bike up and put it on the stand. There was not a mark on me or the scooter but Nick had a black slick all down the sleeve of his jacket and on the leg of his jeans.

Nick – After I had cleaned up in the washroom, the coffee tasted great. In fact, everything was looking good. We had jumped in at the deep end and survived. By now we knew the drill, the roads were beginning to dry, the sky was brightening up and so were we. Apart from a blow to our pride we were doing fine and there was nothing to stop us now.

Nancy – Thanks goodness for wet wipes. They really cut through the road film on the visor.

Nick – So, with better visibility and feeling refreshed and positive, we drove back onto the M25.

10 minutes later, as we beat our way down the motorway, both mirrors started swivelling, independently, like chameleon's eyes. I imagine the screws had loosened due to the constant vibration. It would have been useful if it had happened before we stopped so I could have fixed them in the service station, but that would have been too easy.

Nancy – Nick and I often say that nothing comes easy for us. Everything we do has to be earned the hard way and this is a case in point

Nick – I had options: I could drive on blind – not really an option with all the lorries overtaking, pull over onto the hard shoulder and fix it there, or try and tighten them with my hand as we drove along. I didn't have it in my heart to stop again, we would never reach our destination, so I chose the last option, by far the most stupid and most dangerous! Continuing to drive at 45 miles an hour and using my left hand (remember you can't take your right hand off the throttle or the bike comes to a grinding halt) I twisted the mirrors around, one at a time, until they seemed to tighten against themselves. After 3 or 4 tries, they settled into acceptable positions so that I could just about see behind us. Every so often one of them would slowly creep sideways but then I would grab it and tighten it again. We drove like that until our next petrol stop, half way to Dover.

The scooter came fully equipped with a neat little set of silver spanners. How brilliant and all the way from China. However, after trying them all, not one of them fitted the nuts on the mirrors. Brilliant. I imagined a worker on the assembly line, somewhere in China, with a wry smile on their face.

With a lot of fiddling, and by using brute force, we got the mirrors tightened so that I could see behind us in both, and that is how they remained all the way to Greece.

Petrol was interesting. We filled up and it cost us £4.35. Admittedly we were being careful and filling up before it got too low but at this rate we were going to cross Europe for about 40 quid! The handbook said the tank held just under 7 litres so how far on a tank of petrol and how many miles to a gallon? As we drove on, I tried working it out. One litre is approximately one and 3-quarter pints. There are 8 pints in a gallon so one gallon is about 4.5 litres.

We never found out. To calculate it properly we would have had to empty the tank and then drive the scooter till it was empty again. That was not going to happen, not on this journey anyway. The last thing we wanted was to run out in the middle of nowhere, miles from a petrol station. However, we think we were doing somewhere between 70 and 90 miles to the gallon but don't ask how many kilometres that is to the gallon let alone kilometres to the litre, for goodness' sake. We gave up on the calculation. As long as we were careful and kept the tank topped up, we didn't care.

We soon got into a ritual. In an hour, we drove about 45 or 50 miles, which was when the gauge started to drop below half full, and after that we began to feel stiff and in need of a stretch anyway. So, it was going to be 'slow and steady' all the way across Europe. We reached Dover at 10.30, an hour and a half early but jubilant and hardened bikers. We were the first in the queue of bikes. We had made it.

We took off our helmets and my hair was all messed up. Tut, tut, not like a car. We put the bike on the stand like a couple of professionals and I sat back on the seat to ponder. We had driven for about 4 hours including stops and I ached.

Driving a 2-wheeler is absolutely nothing like driving a car. When driving a motorcycle, you form a rigid triangle with the machine. Your arms, from the handlebars to your shoulders form one side of the triangle, your body from your shoulders to your feet and the running board form the second side, and then the bike back to your hands form the third side.

Unlike in a car, where you can relax, on a bike you can't move. It is imperative you concentrate one hundred per cent, all the time. You cannot take your hand off the throttle, it must be constantly fixed hard back to keep it open. (Why haven't they invented overdrive on bikes like they have on cars? Just press a button and it cruises at the desired speed so you can relax and stop throttling the poor throttle.) Also, unlike a car, you can't move your legs without affecting the balance, you can't really move your left hand without affecting that rigid triangle and drifting off line, you can't relax and look at the scenery, you can't have a proper conversation with your passenger, let alone grab a drink or a sandwich.

(Of course, we never do the last 2 things because we could be fined for it in Britain! And, by the way, we could also be fined for snow on the roof of our car, splashing a pedestrian as we drive through a puddle – my favourite pastime – or having a dirty number plate! Good old nanny state!)

Anyway, perhaps with one of the larger, new, fully equipped motor cycles one can relax a little but, half way between London and Dover, I decided that I would never drive a long way on a bike again. Tootling around my local community would be quite enough in the future and surely that was what they are ideally designed for? For a long journey, give me the comfort of a car every time.

I can hear hardened bikers everywhere, groaning. And speaking of which, as we sat there feeling proud of ourselves, a hardened motorcyclist joined the queue. He roared up behind us, on a 1250 cc BMW. He was German (surprise) and, as he dismounted and de-togged, I gave him a serious nod, biker to biker. He was nice enough to acknowledge us. He even came up and admired the scooter. We exchanged information about each other's machines, man to man. Him in his all black leathers, me in my yellow, all-weather, boating, waterproof coat and blue jeans. He might have looked good, but I would be alright if the boat went down!

Nancy – He was very pleasant. He had been touring Britain on his own and was now heading back to Frankfurt.

He obviously had none of the issues that Nick was having with motorcycles. Maybe he had learnt to relax!

However, it was then that I noticed a red sticker, on the front of our scooter, between Nick's knees which said "WARNING". I asked Nick what the notice was and he said he didn't know because he never used his reading glasses when he was on the scooter. I leant over and read it out loud:

'The speed in the first 300 miles should not exceed 25 miles an hour.' I looked at Nick. We had been topping 50! So, as a hardened biker, what did he have to say, 'Oh well, it's a bit late now.'

Nick – It's true. It *was* too late. There's no point in crying over spilt milk. What could we have done anyway? Spent 12 hours the day before, cruising around London just to burn off 300 miles? Crawled our way across Europe at 25 miles an hour? I think not. It also said, 'Always wear a helmet.' I rest my case.

So, we went for breakfast in the port cafe and put it from our minds. We were hungry, but I don't know why. We hadn't done much.

Isn't it amazing how travel makes you hungry? When Nancy and I set off on a journey anywhere, we get about half a mile down the road and simply have to eat all the sandwiches! What's that about?

I chose a table in the café from where I could keep an eye on the scooter. Like any owner of a shiny, new object, I had to continually make sure no one was stealing it, even though the steering lock was on and the Port of Dover had to be one of the most secure places in the world.

As Nancy perused the automatic chocolate dispenser in the corner, I found an information leaflet. Did you know that, up until 1953, the Port of Dover had to lift cars, and even coaches, on and off the ferries by crane! How quaint is that! Now, apparently, it is the world's busiest passenger ferry terminal in the world with around 12 million travellers a year. Perhaps you did know that?

Sailing Away

Nancy – Suddenly the ship became ready for boarding so we worked out a strategy. I would take the luggage up the pedestrian walkway while Nick drove the bike on, before meeting me at reception.

Nick – I was a bit nervous. I had got used to the roads, but now I was being asked to drive up ramps, over lumps and bumps and turn sharp corners. No problem, but the metal decks of these ships can get very greasy with the constant salt air, especially the ramps between decks. Half way up the first ramp my accelerator roared, my back wheel span and I started to waltz all over the surface. Then I slid backwards. I was sweating. I slammed on the brakes and, after tobogganing backwards for a couple more feet, the bike held fast. I was poised on tiptoe like a ballerina and imagined the worst – the scooter would fall away from me and go scraping and bumping down the ramp, scratched and dented at the very first hurdle.

Slowly, I eased open the throttle. The back wheels slid but eventually bit into the metal tracking and, slowly, I inched up the slope. At the next ramp, I had it all worked out. It was about getting a good run at it and holding an even speed all the way up. I held my breath, and it worked. I suppose seasoned riders know the tricks already but for me it was new and challenging.

I hadn't a clue where I was meant to go next but I followed a motorcyclist who had overtaken me and, when he stopped, I pulled up behind him, whereupon a very nice man came up and fixed the bike to the deck and the bulkhead with straps.

Nancy – When Nick met me on board, he was still visibly shaken. Listening to his story I wondered if I would ever be able to drive the scooter around our little island on my own.

We settled with our rucksack and helmets at an outside table at the stern of the ship and watched as it pulled slowly out of the harbour.

I hadn't realised until now that Dover is just like a big bus station. There is a line of bays where the boats dock, spew out their cargo and then pick up a new lot. As we left the teeth of the breakwater, another ferry backed in to our vacated space, the 3 o'clock to Calais.

Dover castle looked very interesting perched on the cliff above the town. (Note to Nick – must visit Dover sometime.)

Nick – We headed off at a northern angle towards Dunkirk. It was the cheapest route and, if we were travelling on to Dusseldorf, cut hours off our journey time.

Nancy – Slowly the light over the boat improved but, in the distance, stretching along the whole south coast of England, a murky grey cloud lurked over the land. The more we moved into the English Channel the more the sun appeared from behind the clouds. Maybe it was symbolic, maybe I was feeling romantic about heading back to Greece or maybe I was feeling just a little brighter in myself.

The nice man with the enormous BMW motorcycle, that we chatted to in the parking lane, was also there. He was quite dishy so I asked him whether he knew if there was a petrol station in Dunkirk, close to the port.

Nick – Nancy is making a point! As we had approached Dover harbour, there was a petrol station, very conveniently situated on the left and Nancy shouted in my ear to stop. I knew we needed petrol but I was keen to reach our destination. And I hate filling up!

Do you know, filling up your car, or scooter in this case, is one of the most loathed activities amongst the British public? I put it off till the very last moment and have come a cropper so many times that I now travel with a can of petrol in the boot. Recently though I let Nancy pay. I find it really does take the pain out of it.

(P.S. Before all you careful, nanny-staters tell me, I know it is inadvisable to keep petrol in the boot. A car could drive into the back of you and blow you sky high or, in intense heat, it could spontaneously explode etc. etc. Perhaps I ought to wear my crash helmet in the car just in case!)

Nancy – Nick is mumbling on again! Anyway, this good-looking biker was very kind and showed me his smart phone on which he had little maps of Dunkirk. He located one for me and allowed me to look. He had a lovely smile.

Nick – Steady on Nancy.

The channel crossing was amazing. It was like trying to cross a busy motorway. Over 400 commercial vessels pass through the Straits of Dover every day, that's 17 every hour, more than one every 5 minutes, all day every day. It's the busiest stretch of water in the world and to stop them bumping into each other they have a left and right. For a ship travelling southwards, they must hug the English coast and for those travelling North they must hug the French coast. The next time you are taking off from Gatwick airport in good weather, check it out. So, all vessels keep to the right, or starboard, and pass other vessels on the left, or port side. That, incidentally, is the international regulation for avoiding a collision at sea. Nancy and I had a little dinghy and outboard once and…

Nancy – When we approached the French coast at Dunkirk, our gateway to Europe, I must be honest and admit it was not all sunshine but at least it looked bright enough to dispel any chance of rain – goodie.

It was 3p.m. French time. I met Nick at the bottom of the ramp and we togged up in our gear. I felt much more confident as I climbed aboard the pillion. We had a 70-mile journey to reach our motel before nightfall. Even at our slowest speed it should take a maximum of 2 hours. Easy peasy.

But first we had to find a petrol station before our tank ran dry. Then the nice German man that I had met on the boat approached us and offered to guide us to one. He had placed his smart phone in a special, little, plastic holder that fitted onto the petrol tank of his motorcycle, so it was just like a sat-nav. Very clever. Why didn't we have one of those apps?

Nick – Cheeky! I'm not responsible for everything. If anybody, you are in charge of apps, far too complicated for me. And who was the one who left our sat-nav in Greece? And, come to think of it, we don't have a petrol tank in front of us to attach it to anyway, so there!

Nancy – Calm down dear!

My German man was all togged up but not in a mismatch of waterproof clothes like us, he was dressed head to toe in a one-piece, black, leather, racing suit. Very sexy.

Nick – Perhaps this is the time to raise the issue of leather motorcycle outfits. Nancy and I had discussed it because I think she secretly wanted one. She is probably too young to have seen *The Girl on the Motorcycle* starring Marianne Faithful. Even Marianne failed to make her leather bike suit look anything other than ridiculous, especially when she pretended to be orgasmic astride her engine, as she pounded the Guildford bypass!

For me, having dead cow stuck all over my body might be one of the best protections for hitting the tarmac but apart from that, it makes no sense on any level. We could have purchased them for around 300 pounds each, except that we would only have used them for one week before discarding them in Symi. And can you imagine us on our little red and white scooter, travelling at 45 miles an hour all togged up in black, one-piece leather suits.

But there is more to it than that, for me. I have never been into black, especially black leather, apart from shoes and, even then, I only own one pair to go with my dress suit and for funerals. There is an element of the devil in black leather. In movies, baddies always wear black and the really bad ones wear black leather. When I was a boy, black leather meant Elvis Presley, greasy hair, rockers and chain swinging violence. Take Marlon Brando in *The Wild One*, for example. It was a way of rebelling, but the rebels were either stupid, violent or unable to escape their own brains. They were locked into their society just as much as the men in the suits were. The fifties, to me, meant the stifling, closed era of macho society before the '60s burst into colour and liberated men from black or grey. I couldn't wait to leave that element of the fifties behind.

There is a song from "Hair", the '60s' musical, which I rather took to heart called 'My Conviction'. It is all about men adopting the dazzling array of colours sported by most of the other male species in the world.

But maybe the real reason I wouldn't wear a one-piece leather suit is bottoms. Have you ever had a good look at bikers in leather trousers? After a while of bending over, the leather around the bottom stretches and they all look like they are packing dirty nappies, or diapers if you are American. How embarrassing is that? Have a look sometime!

Nancy – Well my German man looked the bee's knees.

Nick – I will say he was very kind, even if he did look like he had pooed his pants. He didn't know us from Adam and he had offered to go out of his way to help us. In my book, that makes him a bit of a hero. We followed him into town where he used his 'sat-nav' to find the nearest petrol station, except he couldn't find it.

We travelled around and around the residential streets of Dunkirk watching the petrol gauge getting closer to the bottom of the red mark with no luck. He was so polite he always made sure he never left us behind. I was beginning to wish he had! I would have asked someone for directions, but never mind. Eventually he found petrol and made sure we knew what we were doing before he headed off to Frankfurt amidst our grateful waves and shouts of 'Auf Wiedersehen'.

Nancy – Frankfurt is 350 miles from Dunkirk and he was planning to be home that evening, even though it was already 4 o'clock European time. We were only going a few miles in comparison. Oh for a BMW 1250 throbbing between my legs.

Nick – Right. Yes. Well, we paid our few euros to fill up and we were on our way. Dusseldorf is about 230 miles from Dunkirk but we only planned to ride to our hotel in Westrem near Ghent before we lost the light at around 8, that gave us 4 hours to find it.

Little did we know we would need all of that and more. We had to follow the E40 all the way, then turn right at Ostend bypassing Bruges and Ghent. (A shame because both are beautiful, historic cities. Belgium is so overlooked and so underestimated don't you think?) Anyway, our motel was just past Ghent and, was on the E40. According to my detailed maps taken from the net, (deep intake of breath!) the motel was on the right, after the junction with the N42 where there was a slipway clearly marked.

But we had had experience of these online maps before. Once, when we were looking for Middle Wallop in Dorset it sent us to another Wallop 20 miles away even though we had keyed in the postcode of the destination. And, then, when we were looking for our holiday apartment on the Greek island of Thassos, it sent us to the wrong end of town completely, where we spent 2 hours searching as the rain and darkness fell all over us. In the end, we only found our destination by taking a taxi.

As we hit the French motorways, I got used to driving on the 'wrong side of the road' again very quickly especially because Nancy continually shouted in my ear and gesticulated in front of my face to make sure I stayed on the right-hand side.

We navigated France and Belgium with ease. The problem now was not the driving, it was finding our motel.

Very slowly, we passed the junction with the N42, looking for a slipway just beyond it but there was none, just a turn into a service station. It was obvious there was no hotel in there and we couldn't stop on the hard shoulder, so we argued over the traffic noise, as we drove away from our destination. Imagine it: the middle of Belgium, a red and white scooter swerving across the motorway lane with 2 old, English fogies balanced on top of it, splaying their arms about and shouting at each other.

Nancy – One 'old fogey' thank you. We were tired. We don't often argue or shout at each other.

Nick – At the next junction, 15 miles ahead, I pulled off the motorway and stopped. We drew on all the information that we had: maps torn from the atlas of Europe, my detailed sketches, the address, and our extensive experience of navigating from the past. It seemed we had 2 choices. We either went back onto the E40, drove back to the N42 junction, turned again and made a second pass of the area, maybe ending up here again, or we turned right at this junction onto a B road which ran parallel to the E40 and found it that way by using our noses.

Lost in Belgium

Nick – This is when we made a wrong decision. Rather than stick to the road we knew and return down the other side of the motorway we decided to take the scenic 'B' road.

Looking back, I really don't know why. I suppose we were caught up in the whole excitement of the trip. 15 miles would take no time at all, especially as we had over 2 hours to do it in and, as a team, we are good at finding our way, or so we thought. How hard could the town of Westrem be to find? We threw caution to the wind.

Nancy – I am quite good at French, even though this was Belgium, and we were feeling confident, having driven this far in one day. Six o'clock that very morning seemed like a lifetime away now. We had survived many trials and tribulations. Finding the town would be easy. The sun was out, the road was pleasant and wove between beautiful fields and Belgian villages. It was an adventure.

Nick – What we didn't realise was that the road didn't actually run parallel to the E40 but was slowly pulling away from it at an angle. After a while, I got the map out again, had another look and found a turn right that would take us to our destination.

But, of course, in real life the road looked nothing like the map. We came to some traffic lights in a small town that looked like the junction on the map but there were no signs to Westrem or anywhere else that we could find. Anyway, we took it and drove down a rather bumpy road until after several miles we came to a larger town, but there was still no sign for Westrem or the E40. We had to have taken the wrong turn.

Nancy – After another discussion, we agreed that the junction we had been looking for had to have been further along the original minor road. So, we did a U-turn, made our way back to it, turned right and continued on in the original direction for several miles. But another junction simply didn't materialise.

We were lost and it was beginning to get dark with, maybe, only 45 minutes of light left. We hadn't eaten since before midday, in Dover, and we were tired and getting cold. Now it seemed like an eternity since 6 that morning.

Nick – I stopped again and we had a 'team meeting'. There were 3 options: we could try and find somewhere else to lay our head that night, so forfeiting the £60 for the hotel, we could turn round and re-explore the right turn we had taken earlier and rejected or, the final option, we could put the bike on its stand, drop to the ground and bang our heads on the tarmac.

At this point, Nancy was very strong and gave us a pep talk, after which we turned again and, at the lights, turned down the way we had gone half an hour earlier. When we reached the same town, still with no signs to Westrem in it, I convinced Nancy that as the driver I should stay on the bike while she, with her French, went and asked in a shop. She was brilliant. She came out confused but convinced that she had been told to drive through the town and turn right, which we did. At this point, the lights in the houses were switching on and looked warm and homely. After 20 minutes of further motoring, we found nothing.

We were in darkness and there was nothing around for miles, apart from fields. Then, 5 minutes on, we stumbled across this bar. It was like a beacon in the night. The lights were on and it was full of Belgian workmen drinking their Belgian beers. The whole thing was rather weird. It reminded me of those early Hammer horror films where the stranger stumbles out of the woods into the village pub, the piano stops and they all go quiet.

As I waited on the scooter, I cajoled Nancy forward against her will, into the bar. I was at a low ebb and entering the bar was something I couldn't have done for the life of me. She was heroic.

Nancy – He wasn't fair, but I suppose I did have some French and it did save turning off the engine and putting the bike on the stand. I hate being the first one to go into a pub and always push Nick in first.

Inside the bar, the Belgian men turned to goggle at this strange woman, appearing out of the shadows, holding a crash helmet to her breast and shouting something that sounded like English. Amidst a thick haze of Gauloise smoke, their mouths fell open and their cigarettes would have dropped to the ground had they not stuck to their lower lips!

Nick – I have to say, as I watched her go through the door my heart went out to her. I felt ashamed. She was being so brave and all I was doing was sitting, hiding on the scooter. From that point on I decided I would have to man up. She had done enough. After all, it is my job is to keep her safe and happy.

Nancy – Nick was being too hard on himself. I didn't want to be the one to ask the way but I was the navigator. Nick had driven all day, concentrating hard on the road and keeping the bike upright and me safe. He had been a brick.

Nick – When she emerged, she looked triumphant. The owner of the bar turned out to be a woman who spoke English and she had given Nancy precise directions to our hotel. Nancy had turned defeat into victory. What an amazon.

Nancy – It takes women together to break through all the crap.

Nick – As we drove off, the landlady came running after us shouting directions – take the second road not the first.

Nancy – We had to turn left, go over 2 bridges and we couldn't miss it! Okay?

Nick – It was pitch black now and we were in a nightmare. We drove out into the countryside again, crossed the first bridge, nearly knocking down a man who was walking his dog in the middle of nowhere, and then came to a dead end. The road, or lane as it was now, sort of continued but it was overgrown by trees, and there were bollards barring access. To our right was another dark lane.

Nancy – I was for continuing through the bollards even though the lane was little more than a muddy footpath.

Nick – I was for turning right and exploring down there first, which we did despite Nancy disagreeing. Half a mile on and the lane led through a barred gate and then suddenly emerged into a blaze of lights. It was the motorway service station that we had driven slowly past, nearly 2 hours earlier on the E42. Bugger!

We had entered it the illicit way by the service road. However, there was no hotel, motel, house of bricks, house of straw, nothing! I drove up to the door of the motorway café and Nancy did her thing. When she came out, she was smiling from ear to ear.

Nancy – We had bumbled our way to the right place except the hotel we wanted was on the other side of the motorway.

Nick – I nearly threw my helmet on the floor. It was quarter past 8, and we still had to find our way back to junction 42 of the E40, the junction we had stopped at earlier, then return on the other side of the motorway before turning off into the service station from there. We could see the bloody thing from where were standing. I wanted to lift the scooter over the central barrier. I had had enough.

Nancy – The man at the service till had given me directions as to how to get to the other side of the motorway but said it was complicated. Then he suggested we risk it and go across the E40 by using the spooky, tree covered lane across the rickety-rackety bridge, even though it was banned to vehicles. Apparently, once upon a time, it was a recognised road bridge over the motorway.

Nick – So much for internet mapping, hotel directions, detailed sketches and our innate sense of direction. At that very point in time, I made a vow to myself – I would never, ever, travel anywhere in or on a vehicle, apart from to the shops and back, without a sat-nav. That is an absolute.

It was ridiculous. Here we were, in the middle of Belgium, 2 mature adults, that I like to think are not too dim, who had completely lost their way and become so desperate that they

41

were about to break the law and drive down a very questionable lane, in complete darkness, across a rickety-rackety bridge, that might even have a troll hiding beneath it. I squeezed the scooter slowly through the bollards, slipped over a carpet of muddy leaves, brushed past fallen branches, turned first left and there it was, the motel.

It was 8.30 p.m. and the host was standing behind the reception desk as if she had been there all day, a smile on her face, ready.

As depicted on the net, the motel was a modern, barn construction, with clean cut lines and ample private parking. The host was all smiles and even had her young daughter with her. She pushed her forward to say hello but she hung back, her arms locked behind her, her stomach sticking out and her face turning bright red. Finally, at her mother's insistence, she whispered in her best English, 'Gooood eeevenin'.'

It was charming. All the previous toil and trouble was immediately erased, like it never happened. We were famished but, as we could have predicted knowing our luck, the restaurant was closed. But, oh, how wonderful, we could eat at the service station which was by foot across the lorry park (any port in a storm!).

Nancy – I insisted on a quick shower but Nick was good enough to delay his until after he had eaten and went looking for the cafe.

Nick – The woman behind the desk had disappeared and all was deserted. Well, as we said earlier, nothing comes easy to us. The way out of the lorry park was through a heavy metal turnstile for which you needed a lorry driver's pin card. Deep breath. As far as I could see, there was no other option but to go back along the spooky lane, over the rickety-rackety bridge, to the service station on the other side of the motorway. Give me a break! This day was turning out to be interminable.

No, I was not using the bike. It was safely tucked away for the night, cover on, chain in place. Beside I had had enough of it and I needed a glass of wine.

Nancy – So back we went, on foot, over the spooky bridge, down the dark lane to the service station on the other side of the motorway. What had we done to deserve this? The gate would be locked, the service station shut, the restaurant closed…but no, it was open. Completely empty but open, and they were serving chicken and chips with vegetables. I also grabbed a delicious looking cake for pudding.

Nick – And I grabbed a half bottle of red for pudding.

Is it 'dessert' or 'pudding'? Nancy and I often discuss this. As if most people in the world are worried about what to call the second or third course of their meal when they can't find enough to eat to keep them alive in the first place!

Nancy – For goodness' sake. We were tired and hungry, give it a break.

Nick – Whatever, ask the Queen. She knows language is important as a signifier of class in British society! I think she eats 'pudding'.

Nancy – Nick! Shut up.

We had made it. The bigger the obstacle the greater the victory. The relief was tangible. Canned music played in the restaurant, so I started singing along, Nick joined in and our voices rang out across the empty room as the Belgian waiters looked at us very strangely. Two English oldies in the middle of nowhere, singing their hearts out.

Nick – I'm not old!

Nancy – Ah! If you say so dear.

Day 2

Nick – Is it only day 2? The motel was attractive and we would go there again now we know how to find it. On the E42, it certainly is not but it is set in its own grounds with safe parking and almost new, which showed. We couldn't shut the door to the bathroom because the bed was in the way and we couldn't move the bed because the bedside table was in the way. The shower was in darkness for lack of a light and there was a door in a wall that went nowhere. However, it was warm and, despite being a stone's throw from the motorway, it was quiet. So, after a good night's sleep, we went in search of the motorway slip road.

The motorway was on our doorstep but we still had to do a 6-mile detour to get onto it. Thank goodness we didn't have to retrace the route from the night before – through the dark trees, across the rickety-rackety bridge with the troll lurking beneath! I think it would have let us pass anyway because our little billy goat gruff was very small, not enough meat to fill a troll, and there was bound to be a bigger BMW 1250cc billy goat following on behind, sometime or other. Enough!

This had been another lesson for us though. Just because the internet map says the hotel is right next to the motorway, with a slip road leading to it, don't believe it.

As soon as we were on the motorway, we stopped for petrol, coffee and croissants. Wonderful. I have always been a tea person, oh how boringly British, but since living in Greece I have found the attraction of an hour in the morning, at a waterside café with a latte, a frappe or even, occasionally, a thimble full of thick, strong Greek coffee, washed down by a glass of water, irresistible.

The day was laid out before us. An easy leg through the rest of Belgium, slice through the bottom of Holland and on into Germany. For those of you who keep an eye on E numbers, we had to drive the rest of the E42, then the E313, E314 and E25. We had done all the hard work the day before. We knew the scooter, we knew the roads, we knew how often to stop and it was sunny. We had about 160 miles to go until we hit Dusseldorf and 6 hours to do it in. The train didn't leave till 6pm but they had suggested arriving early, so the only potential problem was finding blasted Hauptbahnhof station in Schlagelstrabe, Dusseldorf. Yes, the language was a problem.

Nancy – Nick is good at Greek, he has worked hard at it but, as for other languages, he has just enough to get him a beer and find the toilets. As for German, he is still at the stage where he giggles at the word for 'vehicle exit' – '*Ausfahrt*'.

Nick – I had done the usual map from the internet although a fat lot of use that had proven the night before! Hauptbahnhof Station was straight in on the A52, across the Rhine, turn left and '*et voila!*'

Well of course it wasn't. We crossed the river looking for a left turn then immediately saw a sign saying right turn for the station. We must have crossed on a different bridge! I grabbed a look behind, 'Quick, stick out your hand Nancy!' and we darted across 3 lanes of traffic, grinning and waving at all the cars that had stopped for us because they felt sorry for this strange red and white contraption veering about all over the road. After 10 more signs, believe it or not, we arrived at Hauptbahnhof station.

Nancy – The journey had been uneventful, except for the German motorway traffic. Gosh don't they travel fast! They seem to appear from nowhere and disappear into nowhere, just as fast.

Nick – I'm glad you mentioned that Nancy, here's a test. What is the speed restriction on German motorways? In Britain, it's 70 mph, of course. In Belgium, it's 75 mph. In France, Holland and Italy – 130 kilometres or 80 mph. So, in Germany? Well, on some autobahns the speed limit is none.

To repeat that, none – no speed restrictions. Some road cars can reach 190 miles an hour. I wonder if rocket cars are allowed on German motorways.

The question is: does going faster on German motorways mean it is more dangerous? Interesting. Well, 29 people per million were killed on British roads in 2016. In Germany, yes more, 39 people per million died on its roads. But, look at this, in France and Italy 53 people per million died on its roads, nearly twice that of Britain. Of course, goody two-shoes Switzerland, with all that snow, only 26 deaths per million. But what of Greece, not noted for its motorways, go on guess … a whopping 75 people per million die on its roads every year. And we were taking a scooter there!

Nancy – Despite the statistics, we had toddled along at our stately 45mph and had still arrived at Hauptbahnhof station early, about 2pm. We were the first bike in the queue.

Nick – We had arrived, it was a beautiful day, the sun was out, the scooter was in one piece and the adventure on the overnight express train lay ahead of us. We took off our gear and revelled in our glory. How clever we were, how unique.

Then a group of 50 German bikers roared around the corner, revving and pushing out exhaust fumes. Suddenly, I felt as if we had wondered into a Wagnerian opera. They were all helmets, studs and leather. All of them were blokes, except for one blonde woman who was first in line and pulled her bike alongside ours. She had to be blonde of course this now being Wagner. Without exception, they wore black leathers and rode enormous black or grey, BMW beasts with engines the size of a small car – even Brunnhilde, the blonde. I'm not sure I would have been able to hold one up let alone pick it up if it fell over! They dwarfed our little scooter.

Like us, they proceeded to strip off their outer garments and, instantly, they were transformed from Wagnerian Gods of the underworld into men. And, how fascinating, all of them except one at the back, wore a black t-shirt with a slogan on it. This is no lie, there were half a dozen "Motorhead" shirts, several others with pictures of bikers on them with fire coming from the rear wheels and wolves howling on rocks in the background, and others with mottos such as 'Live life fast', 'Born to ride' and 'A life behind bars' (geddit?). My favourite must have been: 'I might look like I'm listening to you but in my head I'm riding my bike.'

Aren't humans an odd lot? Most of us live life in one group or another and work so hard to identify, even to the point of wearing the same uniform. Even those that try hard not to fit in do so in such a way that they can be recognised as a member of the group that doesn't fit in. We guessed it wasn't cool to carry a passenger because they were all solo riders, even Brunnhilde who gave me a lovely smile as she stripped off her outer garments. I wouldn't have minded playing groups with her.

Nancy – Steady, darling, you might burst a blood vessel. Quick, take a tablet.

Nick – Thank you, darling. The funny thing is that most of them couldn't resist coming up and checking out our little scooter. They smiled, often a wry, 'what the hell is this', kind of smile. We were sort of in their club but not quite. We were travelling the same road, so to speak, but not in the same way! I did the same back, pretending to admire their bikes. Weren't they wonderful, weren't they big! Mine may be small but at least it was red!

One of them asked whether it was a Lambretta and I explained that it was an AJS, a British brand, but made in China. One of them couldn't help checking the chrome brake network and then another said, 'Colourful isn't it.' at which I had to reply with a wry smile of my own, 'Well, black or grey it is not.'

They were a really friendly lot and at least they could speak English which is more than can be said for me. I have no German at all. The one biker who wore a t-shirt that wasn't black came over and struck up a proper conversation, talking about our bike and asking us where we were going. It turned out that, like us, he was also travelling to Greece but to tour the mainland. He was planning to drive to the ferry at Ancona so when we told him there was a ferry to Greece out of Venice, thereby saving him 160 miles, he was very interested.

It reminded me of another t-shirt which read, "Hung like Albert Einstein. Brains like a horse." Competitive? Moi?

What I have omitted to say is that, of all these bikers, not one was under 50. So, here were all these hard living, fast riding, bats out of hell and not one of them had died young! Looking at their faces, I could see office managers, double-chinned social workers, accountants; anyone who could actually afford £10,000 upwards for a big bike. In fact, the more I looked the more I realised that they were just like me but in tribal, fancy dress. What a lark!

Nancy – Nick seems to have gotten himself stuck in a siding with all this comparing size machismo. What was interesting to me was how we would get the scooter onto the train. We were parked in front of 2 concrete ramps, one which went up and stopped in mid-air, the other which went up a short distance then curved beneath the top one. Eventually, the train reversed into the siding, tail on and hooked up to the ramps.

Nick – I was a little anxious about riding my bike along the top level of the train with nothing to prevent me shooting off so, when we were beckoned forward, being a gentleman, I allowed Brunnhilde to lead the way. Nothing to do with fear of course. To my relief she swerved past the upper ramp and underneath onto the lower level. It became obvious later that the upper level was reserved for cars. Once on the train, the metal tracking for the floor led us away into the distance, rising and falling just like the floors of a waltzer at the funfair. The sides were partially open but it was a bit like travelling down a small tunnel. The talkative biker had told me to keep my head down and, as I looked up, I realised why. On each overhead stanchion, just where the floor rose, were the scratch marks of hundreds of damaged helmets. I took it slowly, rising and falling. Whoopy-do, what fun. Nancy waved me off like I was going on a long journey. Perhaps she had finally given up on me and had decided to fly after all!

Nancy – After a day and a half on the back of the scooter, with the rucksack stuck to my back, the idea did enter my mind. I had also developed a cold. When we were in London, we had met Nick's nephew who had sat on his sofa sniffing, coughing and sneezing. I remember thinking at the time, I hope you don't give me a cold. Well he did and now I was going to pass it onto a trainload of people from all over Europe who would depart the train in Verona and possibly travel onwards to all parts of the world, taking the British cold with them, thereby passing it onto a new group of people who would then take it further and further around the world until it would probably meet us in Greece on its way back. But I wasn't feeling too bad in myself and I cope with colds well, unlike Nick, who, even if he gets a touch of 'man flu', dies noisily for several days.

Nick – I have to say this is one of my pet hates, the phrase 'man flu', like it is not real flu at all. Only women, apparently, have real flu. It is sexist rubbish. Imagine if men used the phrase 'woman flu' in the same way, belittling them and their condition. We would be misogynist pigs. Grrr! And of course, I am never sexist, ever.

Nancy – Maybe, but it doesn't stop you having a roving eye.

Nick – I have no idea what you are talking about. Finally, I reached the front of the motor rail carriages and parked it next to Brunnhilde and her mean machine. I tried to appear in control. I looked her in the eyes, took her in my arms and kissed her squarely on the lips.

Actually, I climbed off the bike and tried to stand it up while she had already climbed out of the train onto the platform. Then, a man came along with big metal clamps which he fitted onto the floor and overhead beams before attaching canvas straps around the scooter. All very exciting.

The scooter, which by now Nancy had decided to call 'Rosy', even though I thought it was a young inexperienced lad, sat very snuggly on the train. But I wasn't at all pleased because it was open to the elements. A bad storm in the night, as we whizzed across Europe, meant it might get wet – tut, tut. However, when I climbed out onto the platform and looked back, it looked rather pleased with itself. I'm sure Brunnhilde's BMW was making eyes at Rosy. I hoped it wouldn't be too rough with her in the night. I imagined several little red and white scooters in between the 2 of them, the next morning.

Nancy – After dropping our bags in our compartment, I found Nick on the platform. We had 2 hours to kill so we went exploring Dusseldorf station, which was interesting. It spread like a subterranean shopping world beneath the platforms and was very cosmopolitan, very modern and very fast. Everybody had somewhere to rush to, unlike us.

Nick – Germany is an enormous country of 82 million people and Dusseldorf, in the far west, with 600,000 people is a relatively small city. Considerably bombed in the Second World War because of its extensive industry, now, I am sure, it is a beautiful city but we didn't have time to find out.

Nancy – We dawdled around the mall looking at the shops. I searched for some paracetamol for my cold. We popped our heads outside the station to peer at the statue of a man taking a photo which was so lifelike I took a photo of it. We drank some pop and looked at the model railway display going round and around. It even had a replica of the motor rail train that we were going to travel on later. But really, all we wanted to do was get on board the real thing and set off on our journey.

Night Train

Nick – The night train from Dusseldorf to Verona, Porta Nuova, was old rolling stock which carried with it a whiff of days gone by. With maroon livery and cream stripes along the side, to us it was unusual and mysterious. It was as long as the platform and the open carriages for the vehicles were strung on the back. A little of the mystery was spoiled however by the picture of bikers loading on 6 packs of beer.

The steps to our carriage were steep and in the corridor, just inside, awaited our hostess for the trip. She was extremely kind and helpful and, being chatty sort of people, we asked her name. In her Dutch accent, she explained it was Astrid, after the Swedish author of *'Pippi Longstocking'* Astrid Lindgren. I have never quite understood the attraction of stories about a young, ginger-haired girl with ridiculous plaits, goofy teeth, freckles and long stockings with garters that are always falling down but then I am not a girl.

Nancy – I must say I was a girl once…

Nick – No really?

Nancy – and, although Pippi is a strong, brave girl, I also found her a bit weird. She is so full of herself and rather disrespectful. They show an old series of *'Pippi Longstocking'* on Greek television and it is beyond me. Perhaps it's lost in the history of Sweden and the Baltic States.

For goodness' sake, Nick has me going off at tangents now

Nick – Ha! Astrid showed us our compartment and explained everything. All we had to do was to choose between us which bunk we wanted, i.e. who was on top, and she would return to make them up later. In one corner was the washroom and there was a little table under the window. Breakfast was thrown in – not literally! The train would leave at 6.30 p.m. and dinner in the dining car was at 8.30.

Well no, Astrid corrected, it was for 6.30.

No, we had booked it for 8.30 which allowed us to watch Germany pass before our eyes as the sun set, and then wash before dinner.

There was some discussion. She had us down for 6.30.

We were adamant we had booked it for 8.30.

Astrid ran off to check and I decided I was going to put my foot down. On this occasion, someone else was going to have to budge, not us.

The motor rail between Dusseldorf and Verona is currently operated by Trainswenkel, a Dutch company. Motor rails, especially sleepers, really are a dying breed in Europe. It seems that companies are unable to make a profit on them. As usual, it is not about providing people with a service but making cash. Looking on the net I noticed that we were really lucky to travel on this train at this price. It seems that next year the company is being taken over by a German group and the cheapest price for a cabin will be over 1,000 euros, even on the last trip of the season, which is what we were on. So, unbeknown to us, this had been our last chance to make this trip.

Astrid returned, looking worried. I took a deep breath ready to engage in battle. But then it turned out that she was looking worried because she had made the mistake and we were indeed booked in for the 8.30 sitting for dinner. She was very apologetic, we were very grateful, and we were all friends once again. As we settled down to look at the station wall through the window, the train began to move. We were off. The scooter was safely stowed on the back, the table was booked, and our adventure lay ahead. I love trains.

Nancy – So do I. It's a shame that British trains are so expensive. It seems they choose to put the prices up to make a profit, which excludes many would-be travellers, instead of reducing the prices so that people clamour to use them, thereby making a profit and keeping everyone happy at the same time. But perhaps I am being naïve. One of our exciting train journeys was in the south of Italy. It ran along the coast, was new, on time and cheap. Nick and I would love to travel by train in India and maybe China.

Nick – As the suburbs of Dusseldorf passed by, much like any suburb of any European city, Nancy got her tablet out and proceeded to play computer games.

I was astonished. She liked to switch off by playing games on her tablet but surely not now when we were cruising through Germany, into the unknown. Instead of looking at the world in front of her she was tapping pictures of fruit on an 8-inch screen! How could she?

Nancy – Quite easily. I had sat on a scooter for 2 days, I was tired, I had a cold, everything was sorted, now I needed to shut down.

Nick – It was beyond me. I had a go at Nancy, telling her what I thought. I couldn't understand her.

Nancy – And I made it clear to Nick that it was my life and I could choose to do what I want.

Nick – I shut up and looked out of the window.

As we travelled south, on our right, to the East, a massive river appeared. And beyond were fields interspersed with rising ground that changed into hills and then mountains. On our left, by the side of the tracks and running parallel to them, was a road and behind that rose tall river cliffs. This was the magnificent Rhine valley. What an unexpected treat. Of course, Dusseldorf is on the Rhine. The centre of communications and industry!

We had never seen the Rhine before and I was massively impressed. So was Nancy when she drew herself away from "Gardenscapes".

Nancy – For goodness' sake. I put the game away when I was ready and dutifully looked at the Rhine. It was impressive though. It was so wide. There were enormous pleasure boats travelling up and down, all lit up in the failing light, restaurants lining the banks and fairy tale castles topping pointy hills.

Nick – A steward passed the compartment so I asked him the name of the river, just to confirm it. He was Dutch, like all the train staff, but he surprised me by answering that it was 'The Rhine, Germany's great river'. Yes, that is true, but it rises in the Swiss Alps, pours out of a glacier in fact, and, at 766 miles long, runs through 5 other European countries including Austria and France before issuing into the North Sea at Rotterdam in the Netherlands. Compare that to the Thames which is only 215 miles long. The name Rhine apparently means 'raging flow' but, as we looked at it this evening, it was anything but.

Nancy – We both fell in love and vowed that not only would we return to Germany to learn more about the country but would spend some time travelling down the Rhine, exploring its hinterland.

Nick – It would have to be on our own boat, so we could take our time and stop at leisure. I wonder what the prices are like.

Nancy – Typical, he's planning another questionable jaunt!

Nick – As the Rhine glided by and the sun went down, it was time to wash for dinner. I appeared refreshed from the washroom and started to dry myself in front of the window while looking at the view. However, at that moment, the road between me and the hills slowly rose and suddenly there was a bus running alongside the train at approximately the same speed. The bus was fully lit and I could see the passengers sitting, all facing the front, faces switched off as they thought about the day that had just passed. Then I realised that, if I could see them and the expressions on their faces, they could see me and the expression on my bare willy. Well it was too late to worry. One of the passengers, a man, turned and checked me out then simply faced the front again. I guessed it must be a regular occurrence! As the bus gradually pulled away, I finished drying and the moment was over.

The next morning, in Italy, I was arrested for indecent exposure…not really.

Nancy – We dressed in the most suitable clothes we could muster, considering everything had been crushed into the rucksack. Nick wore a grey and white, pinstriped shirt tucked into a pair of light chinos, an outfit he had been saving especially for this moment. I wore a blue, crush-proof dress with a few frills on it that made it look dressy, and some sparkly jewellery to lift the whole effect.

Nick – The dining car was very old world, and through our eyes, very romantic. As we faced the engine, down one side were tables for 2, maybe a dozen, and on the other side of the aisle were tables for 4. The whole carriage was divided by etched glass panels, at intervals, giving the feeling of intimacy.

But thanks goodness we are down to earth and not snooty. The tables for 2 were all taken by couples who had dressed for the occasion, but on the other side of the aisle there were the bikers, still dressed in their biker gear, already on their third beer or bottle of wine. It was brilliant, very real and honest. We said hello to our fellow bikers as we sat down and lots of them raised their glasses. It was warm, friendly and fun. Here we were, different nations, different outlooks, different tribes, all locked together in this metal tube for the night, hurtling across Europe, hurtling through time and space, thrown together by circumstance.

I made a fuss over a bottle of wine, as promised, and then studied the menu. Basically, there were 3 choices for each of the 3 courses – meat, fish or vegetarian. Five star it was not but it threw out a few challenges. We both started on carpaccio, you know, thin slices of raw dead things, in this case beef. I love prosciutto, thin slices of raw pig but had never had carpaccio beef. I don't often choose beef. I can't help thinking about cows, how each one has become so deformed to produce as much meat as possible, that they can hardly move the different cuts around on their spindly little legs. Anyway, it always tastes like tough cardboard to me. But this first course was interesting and acceptable.

As the wine flowed, the evening grew more relaxed. I studied the company, as is my want. On the table behind, Nancy there was a couple who looked like they had escaped from a 1940s' movie. She was thin, about 45, wearing a slinky mauve dress with an enormous artificial flower pinned on her left shoulder, and black stockings. Her hair was black, drawn back severely from her thin face, and she wore bright red lipstick and round, gold wire glasses. Her partner, with his back to me, was stocky but wore an oversized grey suit, with a thin stripe. His shoes had been polished to a shine but his hair was thin, in strands that sat unhappily on his scalp as if it was just waiting to blow away. They could have been fugitives from the film *'Casablanca'*.

Across the aisle were 2 old bikers, one with a black t-shirt saying "Evil one" but he was a round faced, happy looking chappy, and the other with a black t-shirt saying "Leave you in the dust" but he seemed to have left all his hair in the dust, somewhere along the way.

And then there was Nancy and me, 2 odd-looking, English people, wearing creased clothes, and broadening smiles as we became slowly inebriated. The second course was, again, a choice of meat, fish or vegetarian. Nancy chose the beef.

Nancy – I wish I had chosen the fish. The beef was thinly sliced, pre-cooked, served with packet, frozen veg. The potatoes were very good and the gravy just about held it all together. Nick chose the pork but it could have been beef.

Nick – I thought it was not bad considering they had an impossibly small kitchen in which to prepare it. It helped that I was hungry and drank more of the wine than Nancy. Also, I was happy just to be there. As I've grown older, I've got better at recognising those moments that will become memorable and try to savour them as fully as possible while they are happening.

The Rhine continued to swan along outside our right-hand window and we marvelled at the views, praised the waitresses and generally mellowed until Nancy decided that it was time for her bed. But for me the night was young. Not that we were in for a party or anything but when again would I find myself in a dining car of a sleeper train heading south to warmer climes. I ordered a German beer, to indicate my intention of returning, then saw Nancy to our compartment.

On my return, things were much the same. The wheels clacked on through the night, more drinks were called for, a bottle of wine was spilled, much to the biker's embarrassment (one would have thought they would have been deliberately smashing their glasses by now) and I sat raising my glass, watching the Rhine outside and the people inside and generally melting into the atmosphere.

Gradually, people paid their bills and made for their beds, so I began to worry about the next day and headed back.

The cabin was cosy now the beds were made up and the lights dimmed. Nancy was still just about awake but snug in her bunk. I stowed my clothes under the seat in case the hostess arrived with breakfast the next morning and saw my underwear strewn across the cabin. Then I climbed the Matterhorn into the top bunk. Even Nancy woke up enough to manage a laugh at my expense. The night was done, the lights were off and the fields and mountains, tunnels and bridges were free to pass by without us checking. We fell into sleep lulled by the rocking of the train.

Day 3, 'We Next Play Verona'

Nick – The whole journey from London to Symi had naturally divided itself into 6 stages: the first from London to Dusseldorf, the second from Dusseldorf to Verona on the sleeper, the third from Verona to Venice, the fourth the boat from Italy to Greece, then across Greece for the final stage on the boat home to Symi. We had done all the hard work on the first stage; the sleeper was not work but pure pleasure. Now we were faced with the hop from Verona to Venice, not a problem. At 74 miles, we could have done it in one and half hours even at our snail's pace.

We had left London on Thursday morning to catch the train on Friday night which meant we arrived in Verona bright and early Saturday morning. The boat out of Venice to Patra, Greece, was not until midday, Sunday, so we had decided to park ourselves up for the night just a half hour drive from Venice, at Padua.

The train was due to arrive in Italy's Verona Porta Nuova Station at 8.30am but was 15 minutes late. After 12 hours and 600 miles, after crossing Switzerland and the Alps, 2 national borders and, while we placed out trust in it as we slept, it was 15 minutes late? Outrageous!

When we had gone to bed, we had left our little train chugging gamely through the night with the dark mountains of Germany towering above it. When we awoke the next morning, sunlight was streaming through the ill-fitting curtains, begging to be let in. We threw them open and there were flat dusty fields with sunlit vines, trailing away into blue distant hills. Where the buildings of Germany had steep sloping rooves for snow to slide off, now the rooves were low pitched and terracotta on yellow stone farmhouses. This was Italy, land of the olive and the olive skinned.

Nancy – We both slept very well but I think we were lucky. I caught a glimpse of our hostess's room as I passed and it could only be described as a cupboard with a small bed, surrounded by boxes, towels and everything else she needed to service us, the travellers. She told us that before returning to Dusseldorf she only had a few hours in which to clean and prepare for her final lot of travellers. What a job! But at least this was her last trip of the season before she became an office worker for the company over winter.

Breakfast was at 7.30 so we made sure we were washed and ready. Nick was a little slow climbing down from his bunk. No change there. He is not at his brightest early in the morning!

I decided that, the next time we were on a sleeper train, I would take the top bunk. Nick seemed to have more room up there and was quietly tucked out of the way.

Nick – For me, it was an obvious choice. I always thought I was a cut above the rest. That is a joke, honest. When I was in the merchant navy, as a lad, I was on the bottom bunk, and in rough seas I was in constant vertical motion, my bum first hitting the floor below then my nose hitting the springs of the bunk above. I felt as if the guy above was suffocating me. Now I hate being too enclosed.

Nancy – When breakfast arrived, it was a continental affair which means it was not cooked and didn't contain bacon and eggs. But it came in a charming little box containing a croissant, a square of butter, a pie, a cake, a fruit drink, a nutty bar and other odds and ends. It also including a hot cup of coffee which was enough to get us on the road without the need to stop.

Nick – After saying our farewells to Astrid, we made our way back along the platform to the unloading yard where all our train mates were also waiting. Isn't it funny how, when you go on a journey like a flight for example, you start with a lot of smart strangers but end up with familiar looking friends with drained out faces, crinkled clothes and messed up hair.

There were several of the bikers from the restaurant the night before and the woman with the stupid little dog we had seen in Dusseldorf, (where did that dog do its poos and wees over night?)

Nancy – There was one very annoying woman, however, who I had spotted on the station at Dusseldorf. She was wearing an immaculately ironed skirt, a sparkling white blouse and high heels. Her nails were perfectly polished and her hair looked as if she had just left the hairdressers! This morning she was clothed in a completely new outfit that looked equally immaculate.

Doesn't it get right up your nose? Well it did mine especially when I looked down at myself in my crumpled travel gear!

Nick – You looked lovely darling. Who wants a woman who is afraid to get her hair messed up?

Being the first one on the train means being the first one off, you can hardly expect all the bikes to reverse along the carriages now can you. So we were long gone while the rest of them were still thinking about it. Nancy was brilliant. She had studied the map and spotted the first sign out of Verona. I helped with my innate sense of direction keeping the sun at 10 o'clock so we were travelling roughly south.

Nancy – Yes!

Nick – The sun was out, we only had a 45-mile drive to Padua and all the signs read Padua, so when Nancy shouted over my shoulder and pointed manically to the E70 motorway I decided to take the B road instead. I thought it would make a nice change to drive through the countryside and see all the Italian villages.

I could feel Nancy shaking with anger behind me and, suddenly, I felt peculiarly vulnerable. After 20 minutes of driving through rural industrial estates with roundabouts at every 400 yards, when Nancy pointed to the E70 again, I surrendered and headed in that direction.

Nancy – But we still had nowhere to stay in Padua that night so I got Nick to stop at a service station that had Wi-Fi. Amidst the coffees and croissants, I got out my tabloid and booked us in at a B&B on the outskirts of the city. We both made a mental note of the map and I wrote down the address and phone number. Sorted.

Nick – The E70 is a fantastic, pan-European highway connecting stretches of motorway in 10 countries from Spain in the west to Georgia in the east, and to join it we had to take a ticket so we could pay our toll as we left it at Padua. No problem. Nancy grabbed it and tucked it safely away in her pocket. Very organised.

Out of the corner of my eye I thought I saw the number "249" on a large sign, in the middle of some confusing Italian, but I ignored it.

The E70 drivers were the worst we had encountered across the whole of Europe. Confronted by a cute little scooter, they would ignore us, drive up to our backside, toot so we nearly fell off as we jumped out of our skin, then cut us up as they passed. I tooted and waived back at them, always wanting to jolly along angry people. The lorry drivers basically tried everything they could to drive us into the side of the road.

But as the road hummed beneath our wheels and the sun beat down on the fields around us, I switched off and let my brain do its own thing. Then I noticed an earworm at the back of my head. It had been there ever since we had left the train. It went like this:

'We open in Venice, we next play Verona, then onto Cremona, lots of money in Cremona.

Our next jump is Parma, that heartless, artless menace and Mantua and Padua, and we open again – where?

We open in Venice and…'

Round and round it went, stuck fast. It was that blasted song by the rat pack, Frank Sinatra, Dean Martin and Sammy Davies Junior, from Cole Porter's *'Kiss me Kate'*, based on Shakespeare's *'The Taming of the Shrew'*.

'We open in Venice…' argh!

So, when the turning for Padua popped up I was quite happy.

There was the usual shouted discussion, above the road noise, as to whether this was the turning for the north, south or central part of the city but unable to hear clearly and with Nancy gesticulating in front of my eyes I was past caring.

Driving can never be a democracy. It's just not possible. Think about it. If it were a democracy, a carload of travellers would have to stop before every action, hold a discussion to consider everybody's point of view and then take a vote on it!

So, I turned off. Nancy paid the toll and we pulled over next to the car park for IKEA, Padua. IKEA, how refreshing, how exotic and how uniquely Italian.

We had never seen Padua but we knew it had an ancient university founded in 1220 and Galileo was once a teacher there.

When I was reading about it, an interesting fact came to light.

'No!' I can hear you say.

Yes… in 302 AD the Greeks, in the form of the Spartans, decided to invade Italy, as you do, and sailed up the river to Padua. Unfortunately, after a lengthy naval battle they were defeated and then, apparently, just gave up the whole idea. Well, 10 out of 10 to the Greeks for audacity but nought out of 10 for persistence. Italy could have been part of Greece now!

In a city of 240,000 people, how do you find a house without a detailed map or sat-nav? Answer – you don't! We knew it was to the south of the city and that it was next to one of the rivers and the ring road. We did 2 circuits of IKEA trying to spy signs for Vigonovo but without success, so we headed for the city centre. Our thinking was that we could then head south into the sun, knowing we were in the correct sector of the city.

Nancy – We were very impressed with Padua, its history and its architecture but our first task was to find our digs. Safely unloaded we could then head back into the city that evening.

Nick – It was Saturday, early afternoon now, and we found ourselves in Piazza del Santo with the magnificent Basilica di

Sant Antonio. We were definitely in Italy. It was beautiful. There were market stalls and children's rides, arcades and expensive shops but no sign of where we were staying that night.

Then Nancy, being her usual heroic self, volunteered to phone the owners. She had booked it and had the details so, instead of hanging on her shoulder and mouthing things in her ear, I thought it wise to leave her to her own designs and went off to ask stallholders and shop keepers if they knew our hotel. No luck. When I returned, she was looking victorious, again. It was a woman on the other end of the phone and she had given Nancy directions in her broken English. I am sure there is a conspiracy going on or is it just that 'Women hold up half the world', as Mao put it.

Nancy – I had saved the day once again. We had to go past the hospital, the general hospital not the other one, turn right then left, alongside a canal, then straight on until we saw a pharmacy. But where was the hospital?

Nick – I went off again and asked where the hospital was and found 2 answers the same as each other, so off we went: past the hospital, turn right, over a bridge, down 'Gata-something' road.

'What road was that dear?'

Nancy – The woman on the phone said something like 'Gatamala'.

Nick – 'Okay, good!' I said but under my breath I mumbled, 'Never again without a sat-nav.' We couldn't see any road names but we had to turn right along the river, or was it a canal, until we came to a park or was it a playground, then across another bridge over what, Nancy wasn't quite sure, turn left, carry on, how far on was unknown, until we saw a pharmacy on the right. If we saw a pharmacy on the right, I would eat my helmet.

After several U-turns, because it didn't 'feel right', I was shocked when we saw a pharmacy. We did another U-turn and went up a residential road without a name. This couldn't be it. We turned round and drove back down the road when suddenly a miracle happened. A woman emerged from a door and waved at us. Gosh! I think Chairman Mao helped out a little.

Nancy – The way I see it, it was probably Saint Anthony who gave us the help. Anyway, I don't know what all the fuss was about, I had the directions very clearly, and now you can eat your helmet.

Nick – The owner was not the owner, she was out, but we were to come in anyway. No wonder nobody knew where this hotel was, it was in a block of 2-storey apartments, in a residential road, in a quiet residential district. However, when we got inside, talk about style. The Italians certainly know how to do it. It was cool and spacious with gorgeous tiles everywhere and a large, turning, wooden staircase. At the top of the stairs, there was a wide landing, turn right and that was us. The apartment was so big I was surprised we found our room without a sat-nav!

Isn't the 21st century amazing. That morning we didn't know where we would be staying but now, following an instant exchange on a thing called the internet and then a brief call on a little, mobile, hand-held box, here we were in our own, beautifully decorated room with magnificent sunlight emanating from windows on 2 sides. The tiled bathroom was so memorable that Nancy took photographs of it so we could copy it for our own house in Greece.

As soon as we had dumped our gear, we were invited down to the spacious kitchen for a very strong coffee but, knowing what the English were like, they managed to rustle up some milk. The cakes were sticky and delicious and we immediately made ourselves at home.

Then the doorbell rang and, in the absence of anyone else, I answered it with a smile, wondering who this stranger was standing on our doorstep. She looked at me and I looked at her and eventually she said in broken Italian, 'Hello, I'm Lucia.' She was the owner, so I let her in. We went through our story again, the one we had told countless times along the way, about England, the ferry, the train and Greece. As usual, she was suitably impressed and told us all about her trip to Athens.

We retired to our room with our coffees, got into bed and fell asleep in front of the TV, as you do.

Nancy – When we awoke, I wanted to drive back into the centre but even I had to admit I couldn't face getting lost again. Padua would have to wait for another time when we could make a more leisurely visit, maybe in a luxurious, central hotel, if money would allow. So instead we decided to visit a restaurant, the owner had told us about, which was just around the corner.

Nick – But before we did, I wanted to move the scooter into the safety of the owner's parking area. As I went outside, the neighbour was standing admiring it, so I told him our story, then the owner came down and took photos, and then her friend came along and I told her our story…half an hour later the job was finally done and we set off on foot for the restaurant.

Nancy – We passed a bar which I eyed up for a late-night drink on the way back. It was me who seemed to be in the mood tonight although my cold was beginning to weigh heavily. I had been very restrained up to now but the next day was a mere 27 miles down to Venice for the boat at midday.

Nick – Turning a corner there was the Italian restaurant the owner had described.

Nancy – No, really Nick, an Italian restaurant, in Italy?

Nick – Yes dear. It was in Italy and it was not serving, souvlaki, curry, roast beef or Wiener schnitzel but pizza and pasta. It was time to relax.

Nancy – We had a lovely evening. I think we are both fairly positive people and generally make the best of what we have. The restaurant was friendly and comfortable.

Nick – Half way through the meal, a large Italian family arrived, not Greek or Indian or…you get the idea, with children in tow, and we enjoyed watching how they sorted themselves out. There was an older gentleman, who was obviously the reason for the meal, and everyone paid him homage, bringing presents and giving him special hugs and kisses. He was brought to tears of happiness especially by the children.

We older blokes become increasingly more aware of our mortality the more the years pass. All those memories and those missed opportunities. Oh, for the chance to do it all again.

Nancy – The children were very well behaved and the parents gave us a conspiratorial wink as they settled into their meal. The noise level rose, the temperature rose, windows were thrown open and the moon peaked its head in around the blinds.

Nick – I ordered a bottle of red but by the time our meal came, Nancy was beginning to feel under the weather with her cold, poor dear. She had one glass so I was forced to drink most of it myself, shame.

Nancy used to drink more red wine but after a few 'interesting' evenings we realised that she had a regular cycle of behaviour with red that she doesn't have with white wine. One glass and she is laughing merrily, 2 and she can pick a fight in an empty room and 3, she becomes maudlin and falls asleep. A big drinker she is not.

Nancy – I cannot pick a fight in an empty room! Nick has to be present to pick a fight with. But, I have to admit, there is probably something in what he says. For some reason, I like a good red wine but red wine doesn't like me. Nowadays, I rarely touch it but, just occasionally, when I only want to drink the odd glass of wine or be kind to Nick, I will help him out. He will not touch white wine at all, except for Retsina. He says it is far too acidic for his taste.

Nick – Well, if it's owning up time, Nancy is very kind to me in this way. Over the years she has developed a kind of pity for me, an old man who has no defence against a sexy glass of red. I hope I am kind to her in other ways.

Nancy – Nope.

Nick – Oh!

Nancy – Yes you are, silly.

Nick – Nancy had pasta and I had pizza, what else? My pizza was enormous. I always say at the beginning 'I will never finish this' but I always do, usually with Nancy's help. Ha, that's one way that I am kind to her!

Nancy – Yes dear.

Nick – She was also very nice to me that night because she didn't want to have a further drink in the bar after all but still came with me to have a cup of tea. Oh dear, poor thing, she can be so kind.

I spied a very large and cheap bottle of the Italian, Moretti beer. Very nice, I like Moretti's. But have you noticed that the picture on the label of Moretti beer bottles is of a man wearing, what I always think of as, a typical Bavarian outfit – lederhosen and a feathered alpine hat. I always thought it was a bit odd because it didn't make me think of Italy at all. Well, get this, originally the beer was brewed in Udine which was then part of Austria. There was also a dispute between the brewery and a German photographer who claimed he took the original photo. So, now it is all clear!

Nancy – I often wonder where Nick's brain goes when he is having a beer. Now I know. Snore!

Nick – As I said, the beer was cheap but then, looking around, so was the bar. The lights were full on and it had no atmosphere, but it served to give the locals a no-frills beer. That evening it was interesting enough for us because it was set on the road which meant we could take a table in the window and watch the Italian world go by. Fascinating!

I was very kind to Nancy, again, because I only had one beer when I really wanted another 3! We were in bed by 10.

Nancy – So kind!

But, one strange thing happened before our heads hit the pillow. We quietly let ourselves into the front door of the digs so as not to disturb the silence of the sleeping house, but there, seated around the kitchen table, was a crowd of 10 people tucking into plates, piled high with different kinds of food and, every one of them, eating in absolute silence. Because downstairs was open-plan we had to pass the end of the table to reach the stairs, so we called out '*Buona notte*' and waved, but the crowd just ignored us. Not one even acknowledged our presence.

Were we invisible? Was it a phantom meal from another dimension? Were we hallucinating because we were tired? Perhaps we had stumbled into a Bunuel film?

Day 4, Pass the Port

Nick – The next morning, we planned to be out of the B&B by 8am which gave us 2 hours to drive 27miles and find the ferry port while still leaving us 2 hours to get lost. We were even planning it into our calculations now.

We rose at 7, dragged ourselves out of the beautiful bathroom, and went for breakfast.

Nancy – However, when we went downstairs the group of travellers, from the night before, were seated around the same table, with plates piled high again but this time with breakfast food. Again, there was complete silence. Then, slowly, it dawned on us, they were deaf or hard of hearing. No wonder they had ignored us, they hadn't heard us and therefore hadn't even seen us.

They were signing rapidly at each other and when they saw us this time they said 'Good morning' in various ways but all with wide inclusive smiles.

The breakfast was mad. The owner had saved us a table separate from the litter strewn breakfast table of the other group and it was so full of breakfast options that it was difficult to find room for our own plates. Different breads, cereals, fruits, cakes, meats, cheeses, hard-boiled eggs, yogurts, preserves, croissants, cheesecakes. The choice was endless. Then the owner asked what we wanted for breakfast. She was about to cook us anything we fancied on top of the food already piled high on our table. Continental breakfast, this was not! We both declined, partly because we were short of time but also because neither of us, Nick especially, can eat very much in the morning.

Nick – We also had tea to drink. Now, I don't know about you but, speaking generally of course, it is our experience that

Italians have no idea about making tea. Regularly when we have stayed in Venice or Florence we are served up a tea bag with a string on it, floating in a cup of almost cold water. Even when prompted, the water has never come back more than lukewarm. On the other hand, speaking generally again, the Greeks seem to have mastered the concept of boiling water.

Nancy – As Nick and I were in the middle of collecting things to eat from across the table, the other group of travellers re-emerged with their cases packed and ready to leave. It was then that we heard a noise coming from one of the cases. Of course, we realised, they were totally unaware of it. I prodded Nick who was just about to intervene when the owner stepped in and pointed it out to them. After a hectic search of several cases, they found an electric toothbrush still rub-a-dub-dubbing anything in its path.

Nick – That was when that we started to think about how different the world of a deaf person must be. After they had made their goodbyes, all hugs and kisses with the owner, I asked Nancy how a deaf person wakes themselves up in the morning if they are on a deadline. She didn't have a clue and neither did I. I later discovered there are 2 ways, one is with a vibrating mechanism attached to a clock, nowadays I suppose a mobile phone on vibrate mode might do it, the other is a flashing light attached to a clock. I must say neither would work for Nancy. She once slept through an earthquake in Greece.

Nancy – Unfortunately Nick hears every small sound. So even if I turn over in the night it can wake him and he starts mumbling threats to my very life. He is a terrible sleeper. That being said, when we had our first earthquake on Symi, in the middle of the night, Nick thought it was a loud lorry rumbling past on the dirt road outside so turned over and went back to sleep while I, as Nick said, slept through it completely. In the morning, we learnt that all our Greek neighbours had turned out of their houses, as one is meant to do, and we could have been squished in our bed.

Nick – I sleep in the nude, gosh, so by the time I had got washed, dressed and done my hair, I would probably have been dead anyway! I don't like to be seen by my adoring public without being properly prepared. However, thinking about it, maybe next time I could rush outside completely starkers. No one would be able to say anything because it is a perfectly legitimate excuse. Um? I would still have to do my hair though!

Nancy – So true!

We left our digs spot on 8 but not before the owner gave us a pretty gift of personally dried fruit to take with us and some hugs and kisses. She even came out to wave us off.

Nick – First stop the petrol station. Even at 8 in the morning it was not too early for an old man to cross the road and admire the scooter.

We had been given directions back to the E70 – out of the door, turn right, turn right again at the roundabout then straight on. When we looked ahead, we saw the IKEA store, the same IKEA store that we had stopped at the previous day before we went careering off into the city centre and roving around Padua. It was enough to make me spit but not with my visor down. If we had known, we could have saved ourselves one hell of a lot of time and worry. I said nothing about the bloody obvious this time. The worst thing is we actually have a sat-nav in Greece!

Once on the motorway I settled into musing. Driving the scooter can be a lonely affair because it is so difficult to communicate above the noise. But I don't mind. It allows me time to do some thinking, out there, in front, on my own.

'We open in Venice and next stop Verona…' Shut up.

Nancy – It was a beautiful Sunday morning and *my* head, at least, was clear. The E70 was empty, the sun was out and, even at 8 in the morning, at the end of September, we weren't cold. We hadn't seen a drop of rain since we left London. Now we had 4 hours to get to our boat in Venice, what could go wrong.

Nick – Nancy, for goodness' sake shut up. You will tempt fate! What could go wrong, indeed!

As we soaked up the sunshine, shades on, looking cool, the Carabinieri pulled us over. It was like an Italian movie.

They flashed their head lights, overtook and then a black leather glove with a white wristband emerged from the car window and waved us down. I pulled onto the hard shoulder and stopped the bike. Talk about looking cool. They got out of their blue and white police car, pulled on their white caps and sauntered over. They were both very smooth in their Ray-Bans.

Of course, they wanted to see our papers and I knew what they were after. I had guessed the day before when we had first joined the E70 and saw the number "249" on a notice. To use the E70, motor cycles must have an engine size of more than 249 cc's. That is, only bikes of 250 cc's and above can use the motorway. Seeing our scooter is a mere 125 cc's we were breaking the law.

Why didn't I tell Nancy? Well, for a start I wasn't absolutely sure that what I saw was what it meant and, secondly, it was probable that we would get away with it anyway. Thirdly, and more importantly, if I had told Nancy she would have worried about it all the way through Italy, and, what is the use of worrying about something that will probably never happen. Today my luck was out.

Nancy – I suppose it was a good thing that Nick hadn't told me because I would have worried. However, and it is a big 'however', we are sharing our life together and it is our policy that we share everything that is important.

No wonder the day before the Italian drivers were the worst in Europe, pulling up behind us, honking their horns and almost driving us off the road. They must have been livid with us breaking the law!

Nick – So, there we were, gazing at the sunlit fields while the Carabinieri gazed at our documents. They were very 'nice', that peculiarly British word, polite, apologetic even.

Nancy – And so good looking. Suave young men with nice bums and a twinkle in their eyes, behind their sunglasses.

Nick – You would think they would have had something better to do on a quiet Sunday morning but then perhaps that is the point, there was nothing else to do except us.

There was good news and bad news. The bad news was a fine of 35 euros. The good news it was 30% off for good behaviour, that is, for actually paying on the spot. The other bad news, they charged an administration fee on top of that just for writing out the ticket.

Nancy – Ten minutes later and 20-odd euros lighter they very kindly escorted us off the motorway, with lights flashing.

Nick – More bad news. The next exit was only a couple of hundred yards ahead. A few more minutes and we would have escaped the police altogether. Is that sod's law or what?

However, things looked up again. We were travelling with ANEK shipping Lines and, when we stopped to find our whereabouts, there was an ANEK sign on the roundabout dead ahead.

But, and this was interesting, it took us in a different direction to the one we had originally intended to take. One of our friends had told us how fantastic it was, leaving Venice for Greece because you had such a spectacular view of the Grand Canal and Saint Mark's Square. Also, we had done our usual internet research on the location of the port and every site showed our ship leaving Venice from one of the islands.

So, the final good news was that, although the Carabinieri stopped us, had they not done so we would probably have been heading for the wrong port, in Venice itself, with a strong likelihood that we would have missed our boat!

Nancy – As it was, within a few minutes, we were parked up at the correct port and relaxing.

But Who's Driving the Boat?

Nick – Well here we were in the Venice lagoon. It was the middle of the fourth day and in all we had travelled approximately 1,100 miles, half of those on the train. The back of the journey was broken because the next leg, Venice to Patra in northern Greece, all 871 miles of it, was by sea, what a breeze.

Although the scooter is great it's a liability, something to always keep an eye on, to worry about. Now it was safely stowed in the hold, we had 32 hours in a floating hotel. Thirty-two hours to spoil ourselves rotten and do exactly what we wanted. It was party time. This wasn't so much a journey as a cruise. "The Hellenic Spirit" has a swimming pool, a nightclub, a couple of bars, 2 restaurants and we had a cabin with a view of the sea drifting endlessly by. Of course, by now this was the beginning of October and, although it was sunny, the pool was empty as was the nightclub. In fact, the whole ship was almost empty. It was fantastic, we more or less had it to ourselves.

Every time we travel by ship, Nancy and I like to be there to watch the ropes untied. It's a sort of rite of passage. The massive ropes are manhandled over the quay into the water and then dragged on board and the gap between ship and land widen as it pulls away.

I find it exhilarating but sad at the same time. The people on board are travelling to new destinations and new stages of their lives, and when they wave goodbye to the people on shore they never know if they will meet them again.

Nancy – We didn't know if we would be passing this way again. We certainly wouldn't be riding a scooter across Europe again, that was sure.

Nick – As a young man in the merchant navy, I regularly shipped out of Southampton, travelling to Australia on the other side of the world. The handrails of the liner would be full of people waving and crying. They would shout last minute messages of love to those left behind on the quay, but their voices would be drowned out by the hubbub. There would be hundreds of lines of coloured, paper tape, stretching from ship to shore, thrown down from the passengers to their soulmates, and each person would hold an end of the tape as the boat pulled away. They would stretch out their arms, leaning into the gap, hopelessly trying to put off the inevitable moment when the tape would snap and the link between them would be broken. Then the 2 loose ends would finally drift aimlessly away on the wind.

Dead on 12, midday, the horn of "The Hellenic Spirit" deafened us with its blast and Italy floated away and slowly disintegrated into a heat haze. How I love ships, and this one was beautiful. The youngest and fastest of the ANEK Lines fleet, it was a floating castle, averaging 32 knots, while holding 1,850 passengers and 600 cars. It's a big beauty at 670 feet long, about the length of 2 football pitches! Have you ever walked a football pitch?

Nancy – Venice slowly drifted by but, despite our friend's raving revue, it was merely a line of grey buildings in the distance. We think they have either changed the location of the international port or our friend was on a cruise liner, they still seem to dock on the islands.

Nick – We love Venice. I went there first with a buddy. Being fed up with January we booked a cheap flight with an airline that will remain nameless, for £20 each way and then a cheap B&B on the main drag from the station to St Mark's square. When we got there, it turned out that it was the beginning of Carnival week. Aren't all the best things unexpected? It was amazing.

Nancy – After we met, Nick surprised me by booking us a holiday for carnival week again. I instantly fell in love with it, just as Nick had, and we have been back half a dozen times since. To view it from a distance was like honey on the elbow.

We could see it, we could smell it but we couldn't taste it. How much we wished to be there on a vaporetti, heading down the Grand Canal, wrapped up against the cold wind with the snow on the mountains in the distance.

Nick – But of course Venice is in danger. We took an hour to reach the open sea, a distance of about 6 miles, because the ship had to crawl along a special channel, with breakwaters on the Venice side to avoid the wake. But still the ghastly, giant cruise ships float through the city, dwarfing its history and causing erosion and pollution. I personally hate to see them. Why they can't dock outside of the city is a mystery to me. How long before a major disaster like the "Costa Concordia" happens right there on one of the canals?

Known as 'The floating city' or, more ominously nowadays, 'The sinking city', Venice is under threat. Apparently, it has sunk, or the waters have risen, 9 inches over the last century. The 'aqua-alta', high water, happens more frequently every year because of rising sea levels due to climate change (no discussion). The squares and lower floors of the buildings become flooded and the foundations suffer.

But Venice is also flooded by 30 million tourists every year, on a resident population of only 50,000. This mass tourism damages the very environment they have come to see and erodes the quality of life for residents and tourists alike. With more residents leaving every year, it's possible it could become just another pointless theme park like Las Vegas. That would be an aesthetic, historic and social disaster. The real Venice itself is disappearing beneath a sea of bodies, selfie sticks and wheelie cases. Venice was once known as 'La Serenissima' but no more is it serene.

And, of course, Nancy and I are part of this tourist tsunami.

Nancy – But there is change in the air. All over Europe, in Barcelona, Crete and Dubrovnik for example, there have been demonstrations against unbridled mass tourism which asks the question – how do you control tourism without harming the local economy? Enough of the lecturing.

With the Venice lagoon out of sight we relaxed in the stern and soaked up the sun. It was lovely, especially after miserable London – the sun on the sea, the warmth on our skin – we breathed a deep sigh of relief.

Nick – But this was party time so, eventually, I suggested a shower and a change of clothes before taking a glass of wine and nibbles in the for'ard lounge. With little competition, we found a table overlooking the bow with the bridge directly above us. Chilling out, we played captain as we sat and watched the sunny world moving towards us as the horizon ahead remain stationary. Somewhere over that horizon was Greece, our home.

Nancy – Hours passed and we both had a bit of a doze as the sun went down. I checked out the duty-free shop and bought some perfume, I had suddenly run low.

Nick – It amazes me how Nancy can suddenly run low just when there is a duty-free shop to hand and especially when she has so many perfumes already. I have one fragrance which is quite enough.

Nancy – He hasn't got a clue, poor fella. Fragrances are like shoes and handbags, you can never have enough! Nick likes 'Issy Miyake' for men but he calls it his 'smelly stuff'. I buy him one as a Christmas present so he never runs out.

Nick – I explored the ship and all its little forgotten corners. In one of those corners, I found, looking alone and uncelebrated, an oval plaque which proudly bore the name "Hellenic Spirit. ANEK lines. Chania" prefixed by the abbreviation "M/V", which I discovered stands for "Motor Vessel", the common prefix for passenger ships. Around the top was the name of the shipyard, "Fosen Mek. Verksteder A/S" ("Verksteder" means workshop and "A/S" means a limited company). Below that were the words "Rissa, Norway 2001". So, it was made in Norway for ANEK lines, Chania, Crete in 2001.

It is difficult to explain the place of ships in Greece's heritage. They operate just like buses, between the islands and the mainland. Except that watching one dock in Symi is more like watching *'2001: A Space Odyssey'*. The enormous craft slowly positions itself, inch perfectly, for docking, its machines hissing and clanging as it makes slight adjustments. Like *'Close Encounters of the Third Kind'*, there is a bang as the ramp at the stern begins to lower. I always expect a little alien to be standing there, backlit by a bright light! Then from the bridge come instructions over the loud speakers to the passengers as they gaze out of their portholes, having been transported through time and space.

ANEK is the largest passenger shipping company in Greece and started in 1967 after a Cretan car ferry sank with the loss of 200 lives, amid a scandal about safety regulations. On Crete, people from all walks of life, got together to start up this multi-shareholder company to provide safe and reliable transport and connect them with the rest of the planet.

As I stood there on this empty ship, plying its way south down the Adriatic, I imagined it being launched into Norway's icy waters before an engineer came along to solder this plaque into place, and proudly give it a last polish with his oily rag.

Nancy – Come on Nick I am getting grumpy, I need food.

Nick – At the far end of the stern, down some steps, I found the doghouse. Mustn't tell Nancy, she will be tempted to send me there. In Britain, if your pet crosses the channel it must be vaccinated, microchipped and have a pet passport. In Greece, however, shipping travel is predominantly internal, and the ships have kennels on board so the owners can take their pets on holiday or to visit relatives. It is wonderful to see them fussing them or walking them on the decks instead of worrying about them left all alone at home. Sometimes they even bring smaller lap dogs into the ship's lounges.

Nancy – Nick!

Nick – So it was off to the restaurant. This was not a time to argue! A hungry Nancy is a formidable foe.

Nancy – We had a choice of 2 restaurants, the a-la-carte and the self-service. The a-la-carte looked posh but empty. We imagined us sitting there feeling superior but pitiful in our isolation. Not quite us. The self-service restaurant seemed to do similar food and had more people in it. Despite being hungry, I was in the mood to have fun.

Nick – One whiff of food and Nancy cheered up. We collected our dishes and headed for the till.

This is where it got silly. I had been on the lookout for the Retsina but there was not a bottle in sight! The steward at the till, smartly dressed in his waistcoat and bow tie, was totting up the bill when I asked him, in my best Greek, if he had any Retsina. Well, I couldn't be sure whether he answered me or not so I repeated the question, checking my Greek to make sure I wasn't saying something rude. Again, he seemed to ignore me. I looked at Nancy who looked back at me. Perhaps he was a friend of those travellers we had met in our digs in Padua. 'Retsina?' I asked, leaving out all the complicated Greek. Then we saw it. He lifted his chin the merest smidgen. It was almost unnoticeable.

Nancy started giggling which set me off. I looked back at the waiter, pointed a finger at his chin and, lowering my right eyebrow, said, 'Is that a "Yes" or "No".' The waiter lifted his chin ever so slightly, again, but this time he had a slight smile of his own. 'Is that a yes?' I said. Another chin. It's a, 'No, you haven't got any Retsina?' There was another tilt of the chin. 'Okay, I get it. You haven't got any Retsina,' tilt of the chin, 'so I'll have a bottle of red.' We were all laughing as he opened a bottle of red for us. Greek lesson over. We soon learnt that, in Greece, a slight lift of the chin means 'No' or, if you are on the road and meet another driver coming the other way, 'Hello'.

Nancy – I am very quick at picking up mannerisms and, without helping it, I sometimes lift my chin to say 'No' to Nick. He hates it.

Nick – It is usually when we have had a falling out and I can't get Nancy to acknowledge a word I'm saying in the first place. It drives me bonkers!

Nancy – I know!

Nick – Nancy tried the fish, I had 'Keerino brissola' – pork chop to you and me. Greek pork chops are enormous and delicious.

Nancy – I went easy on the red wine waiting for a nice glass of white in the lounge later.

Nick – After a very giggly meal, we did eventually reach the lounge.

Nancy – It was Nick's fault, he kept messing around.

Nick – I settled in with the rest of the red and Nancy found a 'very satisfactory' white. It was 9ish but there was hardly anyone else around. Music was playing and we were not in a hurry to retire, after all we had earned this break and there was nothing to get up for the next day, but it was going to be a long night in an empty bar. Then, as if on cue, several white coated crew members arrived, ordered a round of drinks and began laughing and joking as they relaxed. Most irregular. What would the captain think?

Then the captain arrived. It was his birthday. They toasted him and then began to take turns in singing karaoke songs and reciting party pieces. It was just what the doctor ordered. Even the captain took his turn.

Nancy – But who's driving the boat?

Nick – Steering the ship darling. Have another glass of wine.

Yippee! Greece at Last

Nick – The cabin was comfortable, not that either of us particular noticed. We slept like logs. Nancy, now I know why I married her, left me sleepy in bed and returned with coffee. Outside it was sunny and the sea was still there, and still blue.

As we lay, looking out of the window, I could see the journey in my mind. There was our ship, like a small, metal monopoly piece, speeding down the map of the Adriatic. Off the starboard side was the Italian coastline and on our port side, to the east was the Adriatic coast. When we left Venice, we were opposite Slovenia but now, if we were close enough, we could have seen the myriad of beautiful islands and beaches that make up Croatia. One of the oddest things about the Adriatic coast, that maybe reflects the discord in the area, is that the country of Croatia is cut completely in 2 by a 12-mile strip of coastline allowing the otherwise landlocked Bosnia Herzegovina access to the coast. So, if I want to go from north Croatia to south Croatia I must pass through another country. I was reading, however, that Croatia is building an enormous bridge to avoid the need.

This is the Balkans. After the wars in the 1990s, they are still seen by many as unstable, with ethnic and nationalist feelings running high. I remember when Nancy and myself were travelling in Croatia we were relaxing on a beach when we realised that on both sides of the bay, were the shells of burnt out hotels, legacy of the wars. We were ignorant tourists

Nancy – Breakfast was calling, so after a slow, luxurious shower we found croissants and coffee and ate them on deck. We had all day to loaf about and intended to make the most of it. You can see Nick has gone quiet because when he is left with just lazing about he has very little to say. He is not very good at doing nothing. We walked the deck, explored the upper decks and went down the front of the boat

Nick – The bow darling. The bow is the pointy bit. And it is a ship. A ship usually crosses oceans, is big enough to have a crew, and, what everyone always says, a ship can carry a boat but a boat cannot carry a ship.

Nancy – So, darling, if I have a motor boat big enough to cross the channel, with a tender hanging on the back and have you as crew member, it is a ship.

Nick – I was trying to be authoritative.

Nancy – Patronising, you mean.

Nick – I suppose so. Ship or boat? The answer is: there is no definitive answer. Some people say it has to have an extra deck to be a ship or be over 40 tons weight but the fact is that humans always want a finite answer with everything nice and neat but in this case the argument just seems to go round and round.

Nancy – We went down the front of the boat, took an empty table and watched the world come towards us.

Nick – Unawares, we sailed south between Albania and the heel of Italy, while the Adriatic Sea changed into the Ionian Sea even though it looked the same. We were due into Patra at 8.30 that evening and had one stop to make beforehand, at Igoumenitsa – try saying that fast, the morning after the night before.

At 2 o'clock, we left the back of Corfu on our starboard side and Igoumenitsa appeared in a small bay ahead. We went astern and watched a handful of people leave the boat and a handful join it. This was sleepy Sunday.

The first time we took a carload of essential items to Greece, we left the boat at Igoumenitsa and drove to Athens across the mainland.

Nancy – 'Ship', we left the 'ship'!

Nick – We could remember every little detail of the drive and, from the bow, could trace the coast road we had taken and the mountains of the mainland behind it. Today, though, we were floating in a blue, indolent haze. Islands came and islands went, the Peloponnese rose out of the sea and then we turned left into the gulf of Patra.

Nancy – 'Port', darling. We turned to 'port'!

Nick – For goodness' sake, go back to sleep.

As the sun set behind us, the lights of Patra appeared as distant dots on the horizon. Slowly they grew into the shape of a city and within one hour we were on dry land, signing in at the reception desk of Hotel Delfini (Hotel Dolphin). Remarkably, we found it by following our noses, without a hitch and without the need for a sat-nav. Wonders will never cease!

Nancy – Hotel Delfini is a grand hotel, right on the sea front, that was offering a good rate for one night. Patra is renowned in Greece for its festivals, especially its carnival, and when we stayed before, we arrived in the middle of one. Brilliantly situated in the centre of town for restaurants and bars, we were kept awake, most of the night, by the thumping of a sound system in a nearby square. This time we chose a quiet hotel on the edge of town with a view of the sea. All we needed was a place to rest our head and close enough to a place to eat. The staff were friendly and we fell back into practicing our best Greek which brought the usual mixture of smiles and approval. Like all countries, Greece really appreciates travellers who at least attempt to speak the language rather than those who merely raise their voices as if the locals are deaf.

Nick – Our room was a little tired, but we weren't going to be there long enough to rate it. Because we were only carrying one change of clothes we washed some essential items in the sink and put them on the balcony, in the hope that they would be dry enough to wear the next morning. After rapid showers, we had no option but to wear the same clothes we had worn that day. Desperately, we sprayed ourselves with our smellies in the hope that no one would notice. Nancy used her expensive new Chanel for the first time, not bad, but we must have smelt like a bordello as we went searching for a taverna.

Not 200 metres from the hotel, note the change from yards to metres, we found an acceptable restaurant on the beach, overlooking the sea. Mind you, it was so dark out there, it could have been the Sahara Desert for all we knew.

It is very odd. In Britain, we had been lucky enough to live by the sea for over 10 years. However, every time we booked a holiday, at home or abroad, we chose exactly the same kind of place – on the sea, by a beach and a harbour, and somewhere with a bit of history. After a while, it dawned on us that we both have a love affair going on with the sea.

When we moved to Greece, we bought a house next to the sea, with a small harbour, a beach and a bit of history! Now that we had been at sea all day, what did we do, we chose a restaurant by the sea even though we couldn't see it! Are we boring or what!

It was a lovely restaurant but being out of season, and a Monday, it was completely empty, apart from us. The waiter, the son of the owner, wanted to talk (this must be Greece) and, after a couple of bottles of Retsina, we became garrulous. We spoke to him in Greek, well a sort of Greek, and he replied in better English than our Greek. It is the usual interchange we have in Greece, both sides wanting to practice the other persons language. As usual, he stayed long enough to pull out a seat at our table and make himself at home, and we exchanged histories. By the end of the evening we were great friends.

Nancy – My cold had developed and I was at the sneezing stage. Apparently, because sneezing was once an early sign of the plague in Britain we still say, 'Bless you.' In Greece, it's the same, we say, "Yassou" meaning "Your health". However, this evening, when I sneezed, our host used the word 'Yitses'. That was a new one on us so the poor young man was forced to explain that it was a word brought down to the towns by the old mountain folk and means – yes, you've guessed it, 'Your health.'

Nick – I am afraid we are real Grecophiles so you may have found that part boring.

Nancy – Thank you darling!

Nick – Sorry dear.

Nancy – Because we had been away for 2 weeks we were simply happy to be back and chose typical Greek food to eat, and it was delicious. At last, we were on home soil.

Day 5, The Road to Athens

Nick – You may be pleased to hear that the journey from Patra to Athens, all 130 miles of it, was uneventful. A scenic ride in 2 legs. The first took us southeast along the top of the Peloponnese, for 80 miles, then the second, northeast into Piraeus, Athens, for the boat at 3pm.

It was a glorious Tuesday morning, the sun was beaming and so were we. This was the last journey by bike before we caught the ferry to Symi and home. Three more hours sitting astride, what by now had become, our trusty steed, and that was it, done. We had decided the night before to hit the trail and catch breakfast on the way. With 5 hours to do a 3-hour journey, we took our time getting up and were still donning our helmets around 9, pure luxury.

Despite having a terrible night's sleep in Patra, the last time we visited, we really liked the city. It is the third largest city in Greece and being a university city, it has a young population and thus a thriving nightlife with some really good restaurants and tavernas.

Nancy – Typical, all about food and drink. Patra is the place where St Andrew lived, and preached Christianity, and where he was horribly crucified by the Romans. He chose to be crucified on a diagonal cross because, as history has it, he thought he was not worthy to be crucified on the same shape cross as Jesus.

Nick – I would have gotten onto that. Apart from being Scotland's patron saint, I bet you haven't made the link between that and the flag of Scotland.

Nancy – St Andrew wore a nice blue cloak?

Nick – No, the diagonal cross on the flag silly.

Nancy – I know that dear. I was just winding you up.

Nick – Oh, for goodness' sake!

Nancy – I think we also like Patras because, in Symi, over the summer, we got to know a lovely young woman who comes from there. She is attending university in Patras and wanted to chat in English to improve her language. She is such a beautiful woman, her sunny attitude seemed to rub off on us and on the idea of Patras itself. Isn't it odd how these things work!

Nick – As we left the city, we had a wonderful view across the gulf to the mainland and the imposing bridge that spans the gap. Opened in 2004 and, at nearly 2 miles long, it is the longest bridge of its type in the world. We stopped and had a good look. It is pure white and quite breathtaking in the morning light, but the need for breakfast dragged us away.

It was the first of October, sunny and beautiful at 19C (about 67F). Over coffee and croissants, we soaked up the warmth and watched the poor Greeks going about their work, but eventually we forced ourselves to get a move on and found the motorway.

It was Motorway 8, brand new at a cost of 2 billion euros. When it was inaugurated, only 6 months earlier by Alexi Tsipras the Prime Minister, he said, 'It stands as a symbol of Greece's ability to stand on its own 2 feet' (that is, despite being bled dry by the European banks).

It is a struggle for Greece to pull towards sovereignty again after the crash and Europe's subsequent financial stranglehold. The long-term contracts brought about by the forced sale of Greece's airports, railways, water and energy, for example, means that for decades, money will be flowing out of Greece instead of staying at home to stimulate the domestic economy. Even the port of Piraeus has been privatised and sold off to China!

In Tsipras' speech, if you change the words 'Greece's ability to stand on its own 2 feet' to 'the ordinary Greek's ability to stand on their own 2 feet', a different picture emerges. In 2013, 60% of young workers were jobless but at least that is down to 35% as we speak. That is only one in 3, only! About 30% of the Greek people are close to the poverty line with over 20%, in 2017, living in extreme poverty which means they cannot pay their bills or warm their houses or regularly eat a meal with meat or fish, or even afford a television, according to European statistics.

Nancy – I don't think this is the place for politics, Nick.

Nick – I think that is one of the problems in Britain. Very few of us want to talk about politics for fear of offending!

Nancy – Well you can get off your high horse now.

Nick – But…

Nancy – Nick!

Nick – Okay. Let's get back to the nitty-gritty of our journey.

We made the usual stops for the 2 "Ps", petrol and piddles but then, all of a sudden, we had to add another "P" stop – "the putrefaction stop". My nose was dissolving into a mucus mess. By now I had succumbed to Nancy's sneezes, which would not have been a problem had I not been riding the scooter with my visor down. If you have seen the movie *'Dumb and Dumber'*, where they go over the mountain on a moped and come down with their runny noses frozen all over their faces, you will know what I mean. The warm wind was drying the…well you get the picture. Suffice it to say, we also had to stop regularly to wash my visor down with water from our drinks bottle. Oh, ignominy!

Nancy – What is the matter with you this morning? First you are off on one about politics now you have become obnoxious about bodily functions!

Nick – I'm ill and it's all your fault.

Nancy – It's your nephew's fault. Anyway, I've had my cold for days now and you haven't heard me complaining?

Nick – No, but my cold is very bad. And I have to do all the driving as well.

Nancy – You poor old thing.

Nick – Less of the old!

Nancy – Oh dear, grumpy groops!

So, once more, there we were, 2 odd English people, driving down a motorway in Greece, in beautiful sunshine, sneezing and coughing and moaning!

But the journey could have been worse, it could have been raining. In fact, the opposite was true. At one of the stops, we were so hot that we removed our coats and tied them round our waist.

Nick – I still had to keep my visor on.

Nancy – Patience Nancy.

It was a fantastic drive and the new motorway almost halved our journey time. What I find interesting about this motorway is that they gave the tunnels names. I don't mean they named them after the area it cuts through, like 'The Dartford Tunnel' for example, but after people. One of the tunnels on this stretch was named after a socialist leader and another after a teacher and left-wing activist who was killed in a demonstration about educational reform. Isn't that amazing and quite controversial, even for Greece.

Nick – So *you* are onto politics now?

Nancy – It's your fault.

I usually leave the factual bits to Nick but seeing he is dying from his debilitating cold I will take over.

Nick – Hmph!

Nancy – In the mountains, across the Gulf of Corinth to our left, was the Oracle of Delphi. It is brilliant because, in a dominantly male society, the oracle was a woman, the high priestess of the temple to Apollo, at Delphi. Through her, Apollo spoke to give advice and prophecies. We are talking 800 years before Christ here. She was clever because she would rarely give a straight answer…

Nick – A woman, who would rarely give a straight answer? Gosh!

Nancy – Watch it!

What I am trying to say is the advice she gave was often deliberately ambiguous. For example, she told Nero that the number 73 marked the hour of his downfall and, while he was thinking he was going to live to the ripe old age of 73, he was abruptly murdered by a man, aged 73.

Nick – So if we consulted her today she would say something like, 'Unless you stop sneezing Nick, Piraeus will arrive in a fog!'

Nancy – She might, indeed, but your visor is clean now, isn't it?

Nick – Snot bad.

Nancy – Ah, I see you're feeling a little better?

Nick – No!

Nancy – The Gulf of Patra slowly morphed into the Gulf of Corinth and soon we were about to cross the Corinthian Canal which links this gulf with the Saronic Gulf on the Athens side. 130 years ago, if we were travelling up the Gulf of Corinth towards Athens in a boat, we would have bumped slap bang into the city of Corinth. To continue by boat, we would have had to turn around and sail another 430 miles around the Peloponnese. Today, in the same boat, we would simply sail straight through the Corinthian Canal, a mere 4 miles, and out the other side. Essentially the Peloponnese is now an island!

Nick – If we were in the same boat as the one from 130 years ago we would probably sink.

Nancy – I will continue! The Corinthian Canal is one of my absolute favourite pieces of engineering. When I crossed it for the first time, I was amazed. Seeing the sheer 300 feet drop of the walls and the boats dwarfed at the bottom, fair took my breath away.

Nick – Okay, you've got me going again, darling, thank you. There is a town at the other end of the canal called Isthmia which, although small, is fascinating in itself.

Nancy – For those of you who aren't interested in the more arcane elements of history, drop a paragraph.

Nick – For thousands of years, before the canal was dug, they actually hauled the boats out here and physically dragged them over land to Corinth, saving them days sailing all the way round The Peloponnese. Isthmia itself dates back hundreds of years before the birth of Christ. Alexander the Great, Emperor Nero and even Saint Paul visited Isthmia because here was the temple to Poseidon, Greek god of the sea, and every 2 years, from 600BC onwards, it held the PanHellenic games, one of the precursors of the modern

Olympic games. Apparently, Poseidon the sea god won Isthmia after a battle with Helios, the Greek god of the sun.

Another spectacular thing about Isthmia is that it is at the end of a massive Roman wall, The Hexamilion, that ran across the whole of the isthmus to keep out the barbarian hoards. With a fortress and 153 towers along its length it is the largest archaeological structure in the whole of Greece. Of course, only parts of it can be seen today.

For those of you interested, I can recommend a brilliant book by David Stuttard that links the characters in Greek mythology to actual places and archaeological sites on the map.

Even today the town is not without its marvels. Isthmia sports a very unusual bridge. You can drive a car across it from one side of the Corinthian canal to the other but, if a boat is coming, it sinks beneath the waves and disappears.

I wonder if the word 'isthmus' comes from the name of the ancient town, or the name of the ancient town comes from the word 'isthmus'?

Nancy – Sigh! After an hour, we were driving through the crumbling waterfront buildings of Piraeus. We have had problems in the past, finding our ship in the port, nearly missing a boat to the islands once. (Gosh how surprising, I can hear you say!) But this time Nick was obviously back on form. He remembered leaving the port from a back entrance, the last time we were there, and, before you could say Blue Star Ferry, we pulled up alongside it.

On an enormous computerised sign, the words "Welcome Aboard" appeared in Greek and English, followed by the itinerary. The names of the islands moved across the screen as we read them aloud, 'Patmos, Lipsi, Leros, Kalymnos, Kos and…' neither of us could help it, we both shouted 'Symi', before giving ourselves a congratulatory cheer followed by hugs and kisses. We had made it. Even if the bike collapsed onto the ground in a heap now, we could drag it onto the boat, this end, and off the boat at the other. Unless the boat sank, we were home and dry.

What am I saying!

What a Surprise!

Nancy – What a stupid thing to say.

Nick – Thank you dear!

Nancy – Tempting fate like that especially with our luck! The boat we always take to Symi, "The Patmos", wasn't there. Two weeks earlier it had come so close to sinking they had to evacuate all the passengers.

Nick – Well, shut my mouth!

Nancy – Apparently, 'The Patmos', the youngest ship of the Blue Star fleet, and its pride and joy, was approaching the island of Ios when it struck a reef, gashed a 90-metre hole in its side and started taking on water! It was 1.45 in the morning, amidst rough seas. The 200 passengers said there was an enormous bang and shaking like an earthquake, with things falling off shelves and tables. Then suddenly it was all sirens and life jackets as nearby boats rushed to the vessel's aid. For a few nail-biting hours, until first light, the passengers were stranded and only then were they able to be transferred to smaller vessels and onto the island. Their cars and trucks had to be left behind.

Imagine if the ship had been full, with 2,000 passengers!

Nick – When an embarrassed crew member told us the story, we were stunned. For such a famous and reliable shipping company to nearly lose a ship is a shocker especially upon such a well-known reef. It seemed ridiculous, careless, dangerous even.

I know it might sound like a storm in a teacup to you but maybe it's because you don't realise that, only 17 years earlier and just 25 miles to the east, a similar passenger ship sank and 72 people were drowned! Not a Blue Star I might add.

And there I was joking about it!

Nancy – Nick and I both adore Blue Star ferries. They are amazing beasts, beasts of burden, criss-crossing the Aegean like blue whales, linking people and places, suppliers and outlets. Apart from the lorries, a person can simply place an item in the boat's hold, say at Piraeus, and another person can then pop on board at its destination and take it off, job done!

The ferries are considered such an important lifeline that they are subsidised by the Greek state to ensure that they don't chase profit at the expense of stranded islanders.

Without them what would we do on Symi. No fresh fruit, no food, no wine, (imagine that!), no restaurants or tavernas. Everything comes in by boat. Even water is brought to the island by tanker.

Nick – Many is the time Nancy and I have sat in the port taverna as the ferry arrives. It is a fantastic sight. It turns around in a little over its own length and ends up stern on to the dock, practically blocking the whole of the harbour. The ramp lowers with a crew member balancing on its lip, ropes fly and then it's 15 minutes of pure havoc. The vehicles and passengers on the dock rush to get on and the vehicles and passengers on the ship, rush to get off. The port police blow their whistles and try and contain the scrum while vehicles rev their engines and push forward. Individuals rush on to pick up parcels, motorcycles roar up one side as the cars rush down the other and passengers fight their way up the gangway. First off is the Post Office van and then one or 2 lorry cabs back in to pick up trailers and dump them ashore before going back in for more. The vans with the provisions that we will see again later in the shops, roll off and, at this point, the cars are allowed on while crew members stop them for their tickets and place destination stickers on their windscreens. Organised mayhem!

Nick – Piraeus was a relative doddle in comparison as the ship has hours there to do a turn-around. I parked the scooter next to the ramp and, again, a crew member couldn't resist asking about it, how much did it cost etc. It surely is a looker.

On board, they secured it with ropes. No snazzy expensive straps like on the English Channel ferries, just ropes and a cloth as a buffer against the paint work, doing exactly the same job. Then, dead on 3pm, we inched away from mainland Greece.

Our ferry would plough through the Mediterranean for 7.5 hours, non-stop, until it hit the Dodecanese (not literally I hope!) and its first port of call, the island of Patmos. From there it would hop from island to island, dropping off and picking up, before we alighted at Symi.

Nancy – But, instead of 'The Patmos' which was still in dry dock, we were stuck with 'The Paros' – smaller, slower, 10 years older and with no restaurant. And it was packed.

But every cloud has a silver lining, it was packed with Symiots. Everywhere we looked there were people we knew. There was Sotiri, our neighbour, coming back from the doctors in Athens, and our local Pappa (priest). Our dentist was on board and a good sampling of yia-yia's (grannies) I knew from my local church.

We couldn't go anywhere on board without saying hello. It was wonderful, like we were home already. The noise of chatter was deafening and there was an exhilarating sense of party time. They are a canny lot these Greeks. Not for them the pricey take-aways. They were opening bag upon bag of home cooked food and pressing nibbles onto us.

Normally I would have organised a picnic but being on the road for the last week made that kind of difficult.

Nick – So, generous handouts apart, we had to fall back upon the services provided by The Paros which amounted to one burger bar and a couple of snack bars serving crisps and the like. We had bought a burger from one of these outlets before and, to be polite, it wasn't to our taste. So, I went on a hunt for alternatives and returned with tiropitas (cheese pies), doughnuts and a couple of coffees. We had a 15-hour journey ahead of us and, frankly, they were not going to cut it. An hour later we were still hungry, so it was cheeseburgers or nothing, ugh!

Time for a glass of wine.

Nancy – We were due in to Symi at 5.30 the next morning so for this trip we decided against a cabin. We both thought it was pointless to pay the extra money for a bed we would probably be late into and which we would crawl out of at 4.30, so we made for one of the quieter lounges on an upper deck with, what they call, 'aircraft style' seats that lean back.

Nick – For those of you who have island hopped in Greece, you will know that people sleep everywhere and anywhere – on seats, benches, floors, carpeted corners, anywhere they can lay their bones.

But, isn't it odd how people like to stick together. The ship was busy, but they had all crammed themselves into the main lounges while we had found an empty lounge, 2 decks up.

When we retired, it was late, as Nancy had predicted. I hadn't wanted to touch a drop that evening but Nancy had insisted.

Nancy – Yeh, yeh, yeh!

We spread ourselves over 3 seats each and Nick went straight off. He seems to sleep better, half sitting up than when he is horizontal in our own bed. He started snoring.

Nick – I don't snore!

Nancy – So what was that noise you were making?

Nick – I had a piece of music going around and round in my head and the only way I could get rid of it, and go to sleep, was to practice regulated breathing and concentrate on relaxing each part of my body in turn.

Nancy – It sounded just like snoring to me.

Nick – People in glasshouses shouldn't throw stones. Nancy will insist on falling asleep on her back so that I have to wait until she starts snoring before I can gently ask her to turn over. Only then can I sleep myself.

Nancy – I don't snore. I simply make delicate sleeping sounds.

Nick – And very sweetly too, darling. The next thing I knew Nancy was stirring and it was coming up to 5.00 in the morning. Once again, she did the coffee and croissant duty. She is my 'tea-in-bed' queen and I really appreciate it.

Nancy – If I waited for Nick we would never have tea in bed. He is so slow to get going in the morning.

Nick – That is true. For Nancy, once she is awake, so is the rest of the world. She can go from nought to 60 faster than a formula one car, whereas I need to come round slowly, savouring my dreams and saying goodbye to the characters who people my sleeping life.

Nancy – Having spent years rising for the early shift as a nurse means I am up and ready to go. I have learnt to accommodate Nick over the years and try to be quiet, but some mornings I just seem to bump into everything, knock things over and slam doors, then the sleeping bear awakes.

Nick – As we sipped our coffees, we gazed out of the ship's window. Symi appeared on our starboard side, a dragon silhouette sleeping in the shallows, as the sun rose behind it. We had been away nearly 3 weeks and were very excited to be back, especially with our new toy. It would revolutionise our existence. No more the waiting for the bus or the walk up to the village on a Sunday afternoon because we had forgotten to buy enough milk.

Nancy – We had also worked out that we did approximately 3 journeys a week on the bus going in and out of town. It is extremely cheap at 1.50 euros each way per person. But, add that up. Two people, both ways, 3 times a week – that's 18 euros a week. That's about 80 euros a month, 960 euros a year. That means the scooter will have paid for itself half way through the second year, and beyond that we would be saving nearly 1,000 euros a year! We were astounded when we worked it out! How many meals out is that?

Nick – How many bottles of wine? I can get a litre and a half of Retsina for 3.50 euros, which is about £1.50 a bottle. £1.50 into a thousand pounds – well, let's just say it's a lot of booze!

Nancy – Nick, for goodness' sake you sound like an alcoholic.

Nick – I do don't I. Sorry.

What I will really miss is going on the bus with all the locals. Up the twisting lanes and along the narrow road by the side of the harbour.

The call went out across the intercom for drivers to go to the vehicle deck, so I went below. I untied the ropes holding my bike and joined the rest of the Symi bikers in a huddle near the ramp. The crew member in charge thrust out his hand to hold us back. In response, we throttled our engines, so he turned again and gave us a stern look. He screwed his eyes and then beckoned the cars to leave first. The game was on. When he turned his back, we inched forward, revving our engines, until he turned round again with an even sterner face. It was just like the child's game 'Statues'. He turned his back, we crept forward, he turned around and we all stopped and pretended we hadn't moved. He shouted at us to stay, he turned his back, we crept forward until, finally, he had had enough and let us go.

On the quay, Nancy waited, helmet firmly on.

Nancy – And Nick was being silly, refusing to put his on.

Nick – From now on I was free. Free as a bird. No one wears their helmets on the island except for tourists. So, say what you will, my helmet hung resolutely on the hook at the front of the bike.

Nancy – At last, we were home, after 7 days and 1,300 miles, half of them driven. Calculating that it is 3 miles into town and how often we would make the trip, we had burnt over a year of the new scooter's life in one week. Poor little thing.

Nick – But it had achieved something that very few other scooters had done. It had crossed Europe by road and survived.

Nancy – And so had we. Nick arrived on terra firma and I gave him a hug and a kiss. We had done it, together. Over slippery roads, against battling lorries and bad drivers, in spite of the Italian police, bad maps, wrong turns and bug-eyed mile after bug-eyed mile, we had survived. We had worked together, picking up the baton when the other grew tired. Sometimes we clutched each other tight just to get us through, but we had made it.

Nick – As I held Nancy in my arms, I realised how essential she had been to our journey and how essential she would be on our journey to come.

Nancy – Now he's just getting soppy.

Nick – And of course the scooter had been essential too, but she knows how to take a compliment. She must have received 20 on the way, from French, Germans, Italians and Greeks alike.

The typical one that sticks in my mind was early one morning when an old man came over. He pushed his cap from his forehead, stood back and admired:

'Vespa?' he asked.

'No, it's an AJS from Britain.'

'You've come all the way from Britain?'

'Yes, we're travelling to Greece.'

'Greece!'

'Not a Vespa then?'

'No, it's a Chinese, retro.'

Oh!' and off he went.

The conversation went more or less the same no matter what the language. I wonder if any of them actually went away and bought one.

But here we were on the quay on Symi and, after all that, where were the crowds, cheering and clapping, the hugs and kisses for bravery and self-sacrifice? Where were the banners and confetti falling from the sky?

Mind you it was only 6am, perhaps they would be amassing later!

Nancy – We stopped off at the 'always-open shop' on the harbour for essentials, drove up the hill and down the other side into Pedi our home bay, parked up, unloaded, put on the bike cover, kissed the neighbours on both cheeks, shut the door, went upstairs, showered and got into bed.

As we drifted off, my hand found Nick's as his hand searched for mine.

Home, sweet home!

Just an Afterthought

Nick – Well, we have been home a month now.

We had to make the scooter legal by declaring it at customs in Rhodes and we wanted to register it to gain Greek number plates, to avoid a massive government tax after 6 months.

We made 3 journeys to Rhodes, helmets tightly fitted I might add. We got the necessary paperwork from customs then drove up the Lindos road and got another piece of paper to take down the Lindos Road to the bank in town. They gave us another piece of paper to take up the Lindos Road to the MOT garage (yes, even though it was brand new!), then drove across the Lindos Road to the registration office. Here we queued for 90 minutes and got another piece of paper to take down the Lindos Road to the motor tax office by the sea. We paid the road tax and were given another piece of paper to drive back up the Lindos Road to the number plate office. We were too late, but we knocked on the door and finally got the actual metal number plate – PYP 883 (whoopee!). Then we drove back across the Lindos Road to the MOT garage again and got a sticker to put on our number plate to prove it had passed.

When we finally stood outside the last office, with the number plate in our hands, we took a large breath. It was difficult to believe we had arrived legally now, as well as physically.

I am speaking generally, I know, but Greeks do seem to love their triple paper work, triple stamps, and triple records. However, throughout all the hassle, they were uniformly helpful and friendly even though at times they must have been quietly losing it in their sweaty, air-starved offices.

Nancy – And now, despite me thinking I would never drive the scooter, I have started practicing. It is difficult because I can't take Nick on the back to help. It makes it all too heavy and wobbly. So, I have to do it all myself.

I have been up to the town and back on my own now and once, over the top and along the narrow road by the sea into the harbour town. It is difficult when I meet a car on the narrow roads and some of the corners are very sharp. I stop if there is any problem or walk the bike round if I am feeling a little unsure about a corner, but I *am* getting there.

Nick – And without being patronising, I think it's brilliant. I'm glad Nancy wears her helmet too, I do worry. At last, she will soon be free of me having to drive her everywhere and indeed, when she gets used to driving with me on the back, she can take me home after a night at the taverna.

Nancy – I love you darling but not that much. On yer bike!